Teacher's Guide

PATHWAYS

Reading, Writing,
and Critical Thinking

2

Laurie Blass

Mari Va...

Ingrid W...

NATIONAL
GEOGRAPHIC
LEARNING

HEINLE
CENGAGE Learning·

Australia • Brazil • Japan • Korea • Mexico • Singapore • Spain • United Kingdom • United States

Pathways 2 Teacher's Guide

Publisher: Andrew Robinson

Executive Editor: Sean Bermingham

Senior Development Editor: Bill Preston

Development Editor: Karen Davy

Director of Global Marketing: Ian Martin

Marketing Manager: Emily Stewart

Director of Content and Media Production:
Michael Burggren

Sr. Content Project Manager: Daisy Sosa

Manufacturing Buyer: Marybeth Hennebury

Cover Design: Page 2 LLC

Cover Image: Patrick McFeeley/National
Geographic Image Collection

Interior Design: Page 2 LLC, Cenveo Publisher
Services/Nesbitt Graphics, Inc.

Composition: Cenveo Publisher Services/
Nesbitt Graphics, Inc.

ISBN-13: 978-1-133-31707-4

ISBN-10: 1-133-31707-3

National Geographic Learning
20 Channel Center St.
Boston, MA 02210
USA

Cengage Learning is a leading provider of customized learning solutions with office locations around the globe, including Singapore, the United Kingdom, Australia, Mexico, Brazil, and Japan. Locate your local office at:
international.cengage.com/region

Cengage Learning products are represented in Canada by Nelson Education, Ltd.

Visit National Geographic Learning online at **ngl.cengage.com**
Visit our corporate website at **www.cengage.com**

Printed in the United States of America
1 2 3 4 5 6 7 8 15 14 13 12

TABLE OF CONTENTS

Advantages of *Pathways Reading, Writing, and Critical Thinking*

In *Pathways Reading, Writing, and Critical Thinking*, real-world content from *National Geographic* publications provides a context for meaningful language acquisition. Students learn essential, high-frequency vocabulary, review important grammatical structures, and practice reading and writing skills that will allow them to succeed in academic settings.

Pathways Reading, Writing, and Critical Thinking can be used in a wide variety of language-learning programs, from high schools and community colleges to private language institutes and intensive English programs. The high-interest content motivates students and teachers alike.

The following features are included in *Pathways Reading, Writing, and Critical Thinking*:

- Academic Pathways goals at the beginning of each unit give students and teachers clear performance objectives.

- Opening pages introduce the unit theme and provide key vocabulary and concepts.

- Readings in a variety of academic content areas and genres present target vocabulary and provide ideas for writing.

- An audio program includes recordings of all the reading texts.

- Clear grammar charts present key structures and language for writing assignments.

- An *Independent Student Handbook* and Vocabulary Index serve as tools to use in class or for self-study and review.

Teaching Language Skills and Academic Literacy

Students need more than language skills to succeed in an academic setting. In addition to teaching the English language, the *Pathways* series teaches academic literacy, which includes not only reading, writing, speaking, and listening skills, but also visual literacy, classroom participation and collaboration skills, critical thinking, and the ability to use technology for learning. Students today are expected to be motivated, inquisitive, original, and creative. In short, they're expected to possess quite an extensive skills set before they even begin their major course of study.

Using *National Geographic* Content in a Language Class

The use of high-interest content from real *National Geographic* publications sets the *Pathways* series apart. Students are engaged by fascinating stories about real people and places around the world and the important issues that affect us all.

High-interest reading passages provide opportunities to practice reading and critical thinking skills, while providing vocabulary and ideas for writing assignments.

The topics in *Pathways Reading, Writing, and Critical Thinking* correspond to academic subject areas and appeal to a wide range of interests. For example:

Academic Subject Area	Unit Title	Unit Theme
Health Science	*Happiness*	factors that contribute to happiness, and research on six keys to happiness
Anthropology/Sociology	*Connected Lives*	new media on the Internet and how it is changing human relationships
Medicine	*Dangerous Cures*	technology for building toxin libraries, and the benefits and dangers of toxins
Earth Science	*Nature's Fury*	the effects of extreme weather, and how firefighters fight wildfires
Business and Technology	*Mobile Revolution*	using cell phones to send information from computers, facilitate language learning, and diagnose medical conditions

Increasing Visual Literacy

Photographs, maps, charts, and graphs can all convey enormous amounts of information. Lecturers and professors rarely present information without some kind of visual aid. Helping students to make sense of visuals is an important part of preparing them for academic success.

Ocean Impact

Human activities are affecting, in some way, all of the world's oceans. These activities include fishing, farming, manufacturing, and offshore gas and oil drilling.

Maps are used in the *Pathways* series not only to show locations and geographical features, but also to illustrate historical facts and current trends—both local and global. In an academic setting, the ability to read maps is expected, and *Pathways* gives students opportunities to hone that skill.

Impact of human activity

- ■ Very high
- ■ High
- ■ Medium high
- ▨ Medium
- ▨ Low
- ■ Very low

Charts and graphs present numerical data in a visual way, and the *Pathways* series gives students practice in reading them.

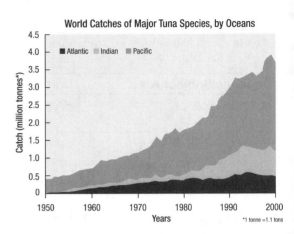

Pathways uses a variety of graphic organizers to present content. Graphic organizers appeal to visual learners by showing relationships between ideas in a visual way. Students use graphic organizers for a number of reading and writing tasks such as note taking, comparing similarities and differences, brainstorming, identifying main ideas and details, and organizing notes for writing assignments.

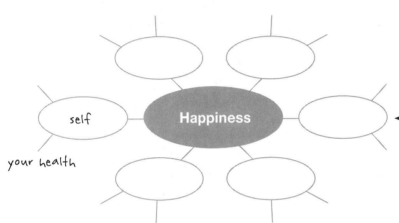

In addition to the more standard pie charts and bar graphs, *Pathways* includes other stimulating informational visuals from *National Geographic* publications.

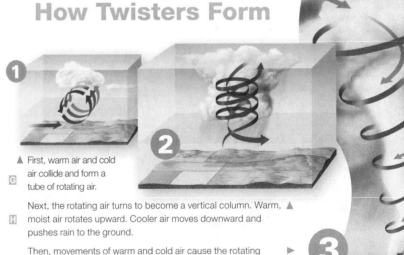

How Twisters Form

First, warm air and cold air collide and form a tube of rotating air.

Next, the rotating air turns to become a vertical column. Warm, moist air rotates upward. Cooler air moves downward and pushes rain to the ground.

Then, movements of warm and cold air cause the rotating winds to form a funnel[5] shape. When the funnel touches the ground, it becomes a tornado.

Building Critical Thinking Skills

Critical thinking skills are explicitly taught and practiced in *Pathways Reading, Writing, and Critical Thinking.* Critical thinking—the ability to make judgments and decisions based on evidence and reason—is an essential skill for students in an academic setting, where they're expected to reflect on and analyze information rather than simply remember it. Students need to be prepared to think critically while listening, reading, writing, and participating in discussions.

The ability to think critically also contributes to language acquisition by requiring deep processing of the language. Having to consider an idea in relation to other ideas and then articulate a response or an opinion about it, involves making complex associations in the brain. This thought process in turn leads to better comprehension and retention of the target language.

Here are just a few examples of the academic tasks that require critical thinking skills:

- deciding which material from a reading to take notes on
- determining a writer's purpose when assessing the content of a reading
- forming an opinion on an issue based on facts and evidence
- relating new information to one's personal experiences
- giving specific examples to support one's main idea
- evaluating sources of information
- synthesizing information

The *Pathways* series gives explicit instruction and practice of critical thinking skills. Each unit has a Critical Thinking Focus and several practice exercises. For example:

D | Critical Thinking: Analyzing Similarities and Differences. In what ways are the structures you read about similar? In what ways are they different? Use your ideas from exercises **B** and **C**. Complete the Venn diagram.

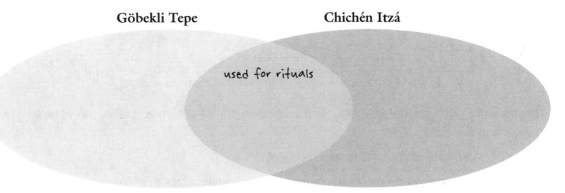

Göbekli Tepe   Chichén Itzá

used for rituals

T Focus

identify
mparisons,
need to
an for and
ect relevant
ails from
erent parts
he text, for
ample, names
people and
ces, years,
nensions, and
er specific
ails.

E | Critical Thinking: Synthesizing. In a small group, compare one of the structures from the reading with either La Sagrada Família or the Pyramids of Giza.

Using Video in the Language Classroom

The video clips in *Pathways Reading, Writing, and Critical Thinking* come from the award-winning *National Geographic* film collection and act as a bridge between Lessons A and Lesson B of each unit. The videos present another perspective on the unit theme in a visually dynamic way. The narration for each video has been carefully graded to feature vocabulary items and structures that are appropriate for students' proficiency level.

Teaching video-viewing skills

In daily life, nonfiction videos can be found on television, on the Internet, and in movie theaters in the form of documentaries. Just as *Pathways* provides a wide variety of reading passages to build students' reading skills, the series also builds viewing skills with videos from *National Geographic*. *Pathways* promotes visual and digital literacy so learners can competently use a wide range of modern media.

Videos differ from reading texts in important ways. First, students are processing information by viewing and listening simultaneously. Visual images include information about the video's setting as well as clues found in nonverbal communication, such as facial expressions, gestures, and other body language. The video may also include maps and diagrams to explain information and processes. The soundtrack contains narration, conversations, music, and sound effects. Some contextual words may appear on screen in signs or as identification of people or settings. In addition, full English subtitles are available as a teaching and learning option.

The Viewing section

The viewing section in each unit features activities for students to do before, while, and after they watch the video.

Before Viewing prepares students for the video by activating their background knowledge and stimulating interest in the topic. Some effective ways of previewing include

- brainstorming ideas and discussing what the class already knows about the topic;
- using photographs and the video's title to predict the content;
- pre-teaching key vocabulary essential to understanding the video content.

While Viewing tasks allow students to focus on

- checking their predictions;
- identifying the main ideas;
- watching and listening for particular details;
- watching and listening for opinions and inferences;
- observing gestures, body language, and other non-verbal communication.

After Viewing gives students opportunities to check comprehension and relate the video to other aspects of the unit by

- describing the main points or sequence of events;
- answering questions to check comprehension of main ideas and key information;
- synthesizing information from the video and previous reading material on the topic.

Some options for using the videos

Preview each video before presenting it in class to become familiar with the content, anticipate questions students might have, and plan how to exploit the video most effectively. See individual units in this Teacher's Guide for notes and suggestions for teaching each video.

Here are some techniques for using video in class:

- Have students preview the video by reading the transcript in the back of the student textbook.
- Pause, rewind, or fast-forward the video to focus on key segments or events.
- Pause the video and ask students to predict what will happen next. Resume the video so students can check their predictions.
- Have students watch the video, or parts of the video, with the sound off so they can focus on what they see. Have students share their ideas about the content. Then play the video with the sound on so students can check their ideas.
- After students have watched the video with the sound on, have them watch again with sound off. Pause the video in different places and ask students to retell the information in their own words.
- Have students watch first without subtitles and discuss the main ideas. Then play the video again with subtitles so students can check their ideas.
- Have students watch the video with the subtitles to help with unknown vocabulary and to aid comprehension.
- Have students watch the video independently and complete the activities in the Online Workbook.

As an optional special project, have students make a presentation or create a written report about a video of their choice, using language they have learned from the textbook and the video narration.

Video scripts are printed in the back of the student textbook. All video clips are on the Online Workbook, the Presentation Tool CD-ROM, and on the classroom DVD. The Online Workbook also contains additional activities about the video.

Features of the *Pathways* Teacher's Guide

The *Pathways* Teacher's Guide contain teaching notes, answer keys, reading and video overviews, and warm-up and extension activities to help teachers present the material in the student textbook.

Ideas for… Boxes

Throughout the *Pathways* Teacher's Guide, there are four types of *Ideas for*. . . Boxes:

- **Ideas for Presenting Grammar** provide a variety of ways to introduce grammatical structures and utilize the grammar charts presented in the Language for Writing sections of the textbook.

- **Ideas for Checking Understanding** present additional questions for assessing students' comprehension of the reading texts.

- **Ideas for Expansion** suggest ways to expand on the content of the book when students need extra instruction or when they have a high level of interest in a topic.

- **Ideas for Multi-level Classes** provide some basic techniques to use in mixed-ability classrooms.

Tips

Tips for instruction and classroom management are provided throughout the *Pathways* Teacher's Guide. The tips are especially helpful to less-experienced teachers, but they are also a resource for more-experienced teachers, providing new ideas and adding variety to the classroom routine.

Suggested Time Frames

The main sections of Lessons A, B, and C in the Teacher's Guide contain small clock icons with suggested times for completing the various tasks. The Writing Task sections in Lesson C do not have time icons because students will likely do writing assignments independently, outside of class. The times are intended as suggestions and may vary, depending on particular teaching situations. Similarly, the estimated time for completing a unit is between four and five class hours. This estimate may vary, depending on how much material is presented in class, given as homework, or other factors.

Graphic Organizers

A set of ten graphic organizers is included in the back of the Teacher's Guide (pages 101–110). You can photocopy these organizers as optional ways to help students organize information as they read particular reading texts in the units.

Audio Program

The audio program includes recordings of all the reading passages in the student textbook. As an option, you may have students listen to the texts while they read.

Following are some frequently asked questions about the *Pathways Reading, Writing, and Critical Thinking* series, answered by authors Laurie Blass and Mari Vargo.

1. How are the Student Book units organized?

Each unit in the *Pathways Reading, Writing, and Critical Thinking* series consists of three lessons: A, B, and C. Lessons A and B focus on reading, and Lesson C on writing. A video viewing segment between Lessons A and B serves as a bridge between the two readings and offers another perspective on the unit theme. Together, these lessons take students from an introduction to the unit theme, through a series of structured reading, vocabulary, and critical thinking activities, and finally through a guided writing assignment that synthesizes the skills, topics, and language presented in the unit.

2. What is the purpose of the Opening and Exploring the Theme pages?

The Opening page presents the unit goals — the Academic Pathways — and provides a general introduction to the unit theme through discussion questions. Exploring the Theme pages are springboards for students to interact with photographs and other graphical information such as maps, graphs, and charts. These pages get students thinking critically and sharing ideas about the unit theme. They present each unit's key concepts and vocabulary while providing opportunities for students to develop visual literacy skills.

3. How are the Lesson A and B readings different?

The Lesson A and B readings present academic content in a variety of genres and formats, and offer different perspectives on the unit themes. This content is adapted from a variety of *National Geographic* sources such as print and online features and articles. The

Lesson A readings are primarily single, linear texts. The Lesson B readings are usually a group of related shorter readings. They represent a variety of formats and text types, including news articles, Web pages, interviews, and profiles, that are linked to each other or to maps and other graphics. The linked aspect of the Lesson B reading texts mirrors a real-world, online reading experience.

4. How does *Pathways Reading, Writing, and Critical Thinking* develop reading strategies?

Each Lesson A presents an academic reading skill along with a series of practice activities. These skills include identifying main and supporting ideas, interpreting visual information, identifying sequence, scanning for specific information, and using graphic organizers to take notes. Students apply what they have learned to the Lesson A reading and then have an opportunity to reinforce the skill in the Lesson B reading. In addition, Strategy boxes appear in various places throughout a unit, wherever students will benefit from a reminder of a previously taught skill.

5. How does the series develop critical thinking skills?

Critical thinking skills are explicitly taught and practiced in *Pathways Reading, Writing, and Critical Thinking*. Each Lesson A includes a specific CT (critical thinking) Focus box that explains the skill — often modeling the thinking process required by the skill through a series of questions. Critical thinking skills include making inferences, evaluating sources for reliability, analyzing the function and purpose of a text, and relating information to personal experience. Students apply the skill to the reading passages in Lessons A and B. Additional CT Focus boxes appear in other places in a unit, wherever students might benefit from a reminder of the skill.

In addition, there are multiple opportunities throughout each unit for students to practice synthesizing information—relating and connecting ideas from different parts of the unit—an essential skill for academic success. Students synthesize and apply information from the video and the Lesson A and B readings, which also prepares them for the unit's writing assignment.

6. How does the series build vocabulary skills?

A set of academic and high-frequency vocabulary items is targeted in both Lessons A and B. Students acquire and reinforce their knowledge of these items by identifying them in context, guessing their meaning, and using them in activities that reinforce meaning and usage. These target words are reinforced and recycled throughout the series.

In addition, Word Partners and Word Link boxes in Lessons A and B expand students' working vocabulary. Word Partners boxes show high-frequency patterns, or collocations, in which target words appear. Word Link boxes focus on prefixes, suffixes, and roots associated with target words.

7. What is the writing process approach taken in this series?

In acquiring academic writing skills, students need to learn early on that writing is re-writing. This is the premise of the process approach to writing, and the approach taken by *Pathways Reading, Writing, and Critical Thinking*. Accordingly, as students work through the pre-writing, writing, and post-writing activities in each unit, they draft

and re-draft their assignments. Repeating this process as they progress through the units, students internalize the steps and gradually become more independent writers.

8. How does it develop writing skills?

The writing section of each unit, Lesson C, begins with a presentation of the writing topic, and then proceeds through the writing process: gathering ideas, planning, drafting, revising, and editing. Students follow this process in a step-by-step manner, working through a series of structured activities. For example, they use outlines and graphic organizers in the planning stage, answer focused questions in the revision stage, and use a checklist in the editing stage.

Each Lesson C includes a Writing Skill presentation box along with a series of practice activities. These presentations include basic paragraph writing skills such as writing topic sentences and supporting main ideas. Later, students move to paragraph organization and development for a variety of genres such as describing, persuading, showing similarities and differences, and explaining a process. Students practice by evaluating model paragraphs, and then apply what they've learned to their own paragraphs as they write and revise their assignments.

In addition, each Lesson C includes a Language for Writing presentation that highlights a lexical or grammar point specifically useful for that unit's writing assignment. Examples include using the simple past for a descriptive paragraph, using *by* + gerund for a cause-effect paragraph, and using comparative adjectives for a comparison paragraph. Students practice the structure in an activity, and then apply what they've learned to their own paragraphs as they write and edit their work.

9. What are some things to keep in mind when using the writing process?

In the brainstorming stage, students work with partners. This helps them express and clarify their ideas before they begin to write. In this stage, remind students that they should not monitor themselves or each other in any way. That is, ideas should flow freely without criticism or limitation.

As part of the brainstorming stage, students write a journal entry in a timed, free-writing activity. This activity should be done in class, if possible, so you can time it. The journal activity is a fluency exercise—that is, the focus is on generating ideas. Accordingly, remind students not to worry about grammar, spelling, or punctuation. The goal is to record ideas in a fluent manner. Do not correct or grade journal entries. If you collect them, you may want to write supportive, constructive comments on students' ideas.

The editing phase includes a peer evaluation activity that encourages students to give each other positive feedback at the outset. Reinforce the idea that students should read their partner's draft first just for meaning and to find at least one positive thing to say about the ideas in the paragraph. If necessary, provide students with some positive conversation starters such as "I like the way you explain X." "Your idea about X is interesting." Remind them of some ways to soften suggestions, such as: "You might want to . . . " "You could . . . " .

10. How are reading and writing integrated in the series?

All the lessons in each unit of *Pathways Reading, Writing, and Critical Thinking* are thematically linked. Lesson A and B readings and activities present and reinforce vocabulary, language, and ideas that students will use in their Lesson C writing assignments. In addition, Lesson A and B readings and skill presentations often model the genre that students will be writing in Lesson C. For example, in Unit 5, students learn to identify cause and effect in the Lesson A passage, review the skill in Lesson B, and then write a cause-effect paragraph. In Unit 7, students identify sequence in a Lesson A passage, review the skill in Lesson B, and then write a process paragraph in Lesson C.

Happiness

Academic Track
Health Science

Academic Pathways:
Lesson A: Identifying an author's main ideas
Guessing meaning from context
Lesson B: Understanding a classification text
Lesson C: Introduction to the paragraph
Writing a topic sentence

Unit Theme

Many people around the world say they want to be happy, but what do they mean by happiness? Does happiness mean the same thing to everyone?

Unit 1 explores the topic of happiness as it relates to:

– the lives of people in Singapore and Mexico
– longevity
– ways to become happier
– evaluating happiness in your community

Think and Discuss (page 1)

- Ask students to describe the picture. What does the picture make them think of? (Possible answers: A happy childhood memory. A time when something made them, or a family member or friend, happy.) Share a personal memory as an example if needed. Do students think children are happier than adults? Why, or why not?

- Discuss question 1 as a class. As a way to model and organize students' responses, you can create a word web. Write the words *To be happy means . . .* on the board and circle them. Then draw several lines from the circle and write students' answers to the question. (Possible answers: having a loving family, having good friends, having a lot of of money, living in a beautiful environment, etc.)

- Discuss question 2. Ask volunteers to tell the class about the person they chose. (Possible answers: Someone who laughs a lot, has a lot of friends, etc.)

Exploring the Theme

(pages 2–3)

The opening spread features information about two happiness surveys.

- Before answering questions 1–3, ask students how they would create a survey to measure people's happiness. What questions would they ask?

- Ask students to look at the first survey. What reasons do they think people in these six countries might have for being happy? Check their understanding of GDP (Gross Domestic Product)

and pc (per capita, or per person), and how this is calculated (GDP pc the total value of goods and services produced by a country, divided by the number of people). Ask why GDP might be higher in some countries than in others.

- Ask students how the second survey is different from the first survey. (The first survey asked people to rate their personal happiness. The second survey included the average life expectancy and environmental impact of people in the countries.)

- Discuss questions 1–3 and compare answers.

Answer Key

1. Costa Rica was the happiest place in both surveys.

2. Possible answers: warm climate (Costa Rica), high GDP pc (Switzerland), low environmental impact (all countries in survey 2)

3. Possible answers: amount of free time, number of people who enjoy their job

TIP For question 3, have students work in groups and develop a happiness survey. Compare the results. Students could survey their friends for homework.

IDEAS FOR... Expansion

Ask students to work individually to write 10 ways to finish the sentence: **Happiness is . . .** Then have them work in groups to choose the best sentences to make a poem about the meaning of happiness.

Preparing to Read *(page 4)*

30 mins

WARM-UP

The Lesson A target vocabulary is presented in the context of comparing happiness for people in Singapore and Mexico.

Ask students what they know about life in Singapore and in Mexico. Why do they think people there might be happy? Brainstorm possible answers and write them on the board. (Possible answers: hot climate, good family relationships, good economy, etc.)

Exercise A. | Building Vocabulary

- Ask students to read the words in the box, and check (✓) the words they know and underline the ones they aren't sure about.
- Have students find the words they don't know in the reading, and use the other words around them to guess their meanings. Then have them complete the sentences using the words in the box.
- Check the answers by asking volunteers to read out a sentence each.
- Point out the **Word Link** box. Discuss the meanings of the abbreviations for word forms and find other forms for some of the words in exercise **A**. (Possible answers: (*n.*) society; (*adj.*) sociable; (*adj.*) accessible)

Vocabulary Notes

The word *access* often appears in the phrase *have access to*. (Many people have access to the Internet through computers and smart phones.) *Confident* and *secure* both describe feelings. Confident means you feel sure about something. (My brother was confident he would pass the test.) Secure means you feel safe. (Having a dog at home makes some people feel secure.)

TIP Review some ways to use the context to guess the meaning of an unfamiliar word. Give an example, using the word *socialize*, the answer to item 1 in Exercise A. The suffix and its position in the sentence in the reading indicate that socialize is a verb. Clues in the previous sentence define *socializing* as talking with a neighbor or having dinner with friends, which means it is something done for fun—as in the context of item 1.

Answer Key

1. socialize
2. poverty
3. access
4. freedom
5. provides
6. standard of living
7. financial
8. secure
9. basic necessities
10. confident

IDEAS FOR... Checking Comprehension

1. How does the government in Singapore help people who are unemployed?
2. How does it help people with low income?
3. How does it help people who look after aging parents?
4. How does this affect the happiness of people in Singapore?
5. What problems do people in Mexico have?
6. How do people in Mexico stay happy?

Exercise B. | Using Vocabulary

Invite volunteers to share their answers with the class. (Possible answers to question 1: good health, a warm home in winter, a job, clean water)

Exercise C. | Brainstorming

- After completing their answers individually, have students compare answers in pairs.
- Make a list on the board and ask the class to choose the six most important things. (Possible answers: good health, good friends, an interesting job, enough money, etc.)

Exercise D. | Predicting

- Draw attention to the reading **Strategy** box. Explain that students will apply this strategy to the reading.
- Explain that predicting is trying to guess the gist, or general idea, of the reading passage—what the most important idea is. Ask students to describe the pictures, and then read out the title and the subheads. Explain that *recipe* in the title does not mean a recipe for how to make food, but a recipe for how to be happy. (The title of this reading is: *Is There a Recipe for Happiness?* The subheads are: *Safety and Security; Friends and Neighbors; A Mixed Recipe?*)
- Ask students to use the pictures, title, and subheads to predict, or guess, what the reading is about. Have them read the captions and say which two countries the passage focuses on. Write their prediction(s) on the board.
- Note: Students will check their prediction(s) later, in exercise **A** on page 7.

track **1-01**

Ask students to read the passage. (Option: Have students listen to the audio as they read.) Explain that the vocabulary definitions in the footnotes at the bottom of page 5 will help them understand the reading.

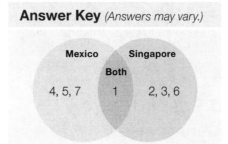

IDEAS FOR... Checking Comprehension

Advise students to start a vocabulary notebook. Demonstrate on the board how to write new words in the notebook, writing different forms for each new word. Ask students for suggestions about what information to include. For example, they might include translations, example sentences, or collocations (words that commonly appear together).

Overview of the Reading

The passage is adapted from Dan Buettner's book *Thrive: Finding Happiness the Blue Zones Way*. The passage presents two contrasting case studies, Singapore and Mexico, which help to make the point that there is no single secret to happiness. The gist, or general idea of the passage, is that there is no simple reason or recipe that explains why people are happy. The passage points out that work, security, safety, freedom, and socializing with friends and family can all play important roles, but there is no single answer that is true for everyone. You can find out more about Dan Buettner's research on: http://www.bluezones.com/about/

Understanding the Reading
(page 7)

Exercise A. | Understanding the Gist

Check students' prediction(s) in exercise **D** on page 4. Did they guess the general idea correctly?

Answer Key

The correct answer is item a. *Security* (item b) is not the most important thing for everyone (*Friends and Neighbors* are also important). The third subhead A Mixed Recipe? indicates that everyone may not need the same basic things to be happy (as stated in item c).

Vocabulary Notes

roughly (paragraph C) = approximately
tops up (paragraph C) = adds value, increases
What matters more (paragraph G) = What's more important

Exercise B. | Identifying Key Details

- Explain that a Venn diagram, like the one on page 7, is a useful way to compare two (or more) things, to

show how they are alike and different. In this case, the diagram is used to show which characteristics apply to people in Singapore vs. Mexico, and which characteristics they share.
- Explain that students should write the number of each statement in one of the three parts of the diagram: in the left circle if it applies only to Mexico, in the right circle if it applies only to Singapore, and in the middle if it applies to both.
- Draw the diagram on the board and ask students to tell you the answers as you write them in the diagram.

Answer Key *(Answers may vary.)*

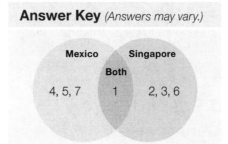

Mexico	Both	Singapore
4, 5, 7	1	2, 3, 6

Exercise C. | Critical Thinking: Guessing Meaning from Context

- Draw students' attention to the **CT Focus** box. Discuss why it is important to use context clues and not to rely on a dictionary. (Often the dictionary has several definitions for a word and the context will tell you which one is correct. Also, there can be special meanings of a word in context that do not appear in a dictionary.)
- Ask students to cover the second column.
- Read aloud the sentence stems in the first column. For each one, ask volunteers to explain or define the meaning by using clues in the context of the reading. Note that all the items refer to the first part of the reading (page 5). Accept all answers.
- Ask students to uncover the second column and write their answers.

Answer Key

1. c (paragraph B) **3.** d (paragraph C) **5.** a (paragraph D)
2. e (paragraph B) **4.** b (paragraph C)

Exercise D. | Critical Thinking: Analyzing

Ask students to find details in the reading to support their opinions.

Exercise E. | Personalizing

When students finish writing their sentences, discuss them as a class, comparing answers and opinions.

> **IDEAS FOR...   Checking Comprehension**
>
> Ask students to find two facts in the passage that are true about people where they live, and two facts that are not true.

Developing Reading Skills

(page 8)

45 mins

Reading Skill: Identifying the Main Idea

- Ask students to cover the lower part of the box and read the paragraph.
- Ask for suggestions for the main idea.
- Have students uncover the answer choices and choose the answer.
- Check comprehension by asking why items a and b are not main ideas. (They relate to vitamin D and endorphins, which are details/examples.)

Exercise A. | Matching

Ask students to compare answers in pairs, or check them as a class.

Exercise B. | Identifying the Main Idea

track 1-02

- Draw students' attention to the **CT Focus** box. Ask students to explain how they would guess the meaning of the three words in the paragraph by using the context. Give an example for the first word, *fit*. Explain how *unhealthy* relates to the phrase *hard to be happy* in the first sentence, which makes a connection between health and happiness. Therefore, Danish people are happy because they are healthy—or fit.
- Ask students to look at the picture, read the caption, and guess why many people are riding bicycles on this road. Ask if many people use bicycles for transportation where they live, and if there are special bike lanes.

- Allow time for students to read and write their ideas individually. (Option: Have students listen to the audio as they read.)
- Ask for suggestions for the main idea, and try to agree on the best answer.

Viewing: Longevity Leaders
(page 9)

Overview of the Video

Dan Buettner is the author of the books *Thrive: Finding Happiness the Blue Zones Way* and *The Blue Zones: Lessons for Living Longer from the People Who've Lived the Longest.* He and a group of researchers traveled around the world to investigate what factors enable people to live longer. They identified the world's "Blue Zones," communities whose elders live to a record-setting age.

The video describes how the number of elderly people in the world is growing, and it investigates factors that enable people in two places, Sardinia and Okinawa, to live to a very old age.

You can find out about nine common diet and lifestyle habits that keep people living past the age of 100 by searching Dan Buettner under Speakers on this website: www.ted.com/

Vocabulary Notes

roughly = approximately
locally grown = grown in the local area
processed food = food that is produced in factories with artificial added ingredients, e.g., canned food, frozen pizza, sausage
globalization = cultures becoming more similar to each other

Before Viewing

Exercise A. | Guessing Meaning from Context

- Ask students to look at the picture and suggest reasons why some people live longer in some parts of the world. (Possible answers: They are active—walk, exercise—live in a clean/healthy environment.)

- Have students work in pairs to discuss and write definitions of the words. You could do the first one as an example by writing *centenarians* on the board and asking students to complete the definition: *people who live to be 100 years old or older.*

- Compare answers as a class.

Answer Key

1. *centenarians* = people who are 100 years old or older
2. *longevity* = a long life
3. *processed foods* = foods that are not natural or healthy
4. *traditional lifestyle* = people who do things the same way that people have done them for a long time
5. *active* = exercising, playing games, interacting with people

Exercise B. | Brainstorming

Ask volunteers to write their ideas on the board. (Possible answers: drink tea, exercise, don't eat processed foods, spend time with friends)

While Viewing

Exercises A and B.

- Ask students to read the questions in **A** and **B**.
- Play the video. Ask students to check their answers to the Brainstorming exercise in Before Viewing, and to write short answers to questions 1–3 in exercise **B**.

Answer Key

1. seven billion, nine billion
2. Populations in places like the United States, Europe, and China are getting much older, much faster. People have more access to good medical care.
3. The traditional lifestyles of many centenarians are disappearing. Many younger people are less active and eat more processed food. As younger people grow older, they will replace the older, traditional centenarians. People will continue to look to medical science to help live longer lives, instead of following the traditional lifestyles of centenarians, who eat healthy and stay active.

After Viewing

Exercise A.

- Have students discuss and compare answers.
- Play the video again and check the answers.

Exercise B. | Critical Thinking: Synthesizing

Have students work in pairs, referring back to the reading as necessary, and then discuss the answers as a class.

Answer Key *(Answers may vary.)*

They enjoy life, and they have the support of friends and family.

30 mins

Preparing to Read (pages 10–11)

WARM-UP

The Lesson B target vocabulary is presented in the context of what people need to become happier.

Ask students to name three things that they would need to become happier. (Possible answers: more free time, more money, more friends) Write all their suggestions on the board.

Exercise A. | Building Vocabulary

- Ask students to choose if they want to work individually or in pairs.

- Explain that the words in blue are the new vocabulary words and that students should choose which meaning is correct by looking at the context clues here and in the reading.

- Point out the **CT Focus** box. Do the first item together with the class as an example. (The key word *studies* appears in item 1 and in definition a.)

- Point out the **Word Partners** box. Explain that some words, like *factor*, often occur together with other words in speech and writing, as in the examples here: *contributing factor, deciding factor*, etc. Another example is in item 2: the word *goals* is often used with other words, as in *long-term goals, short-term goals, immediate goals*, etc. Explain that learning word partners can help students expand vocabulary. These word partners are sometimes called collocations.

Answer Key

1. a 2. a 3. a 4. b 5. a 6. a 7. b 8. b 9. a 10. a

Exercise B. | Using Vocabulary

- Give an example of your own goals for the first item if necessary.

- Ask students to work in pairs to compare answers when they are finished.

- Ask volunteers to read out their sentences.

- Take notes of any common errors and provide feedback.

IDEAS FOR... Expansion

For exercise **B**, you may want to contrast pairs of words with similar or opposite meanings. Ask students to give examples of each and try to provide a definition. For example:

1. long-term / short-term
2. community / neighborhood
3. hobby / sport
4. grateful / ungrateful

Example:

T: What is the difference between a long-term and a short-term goal?
S: A short-term goal is for today or this week. A long-term goal is for next year or for two years from now.
T: Very good. Can you give me some examples?

Exercise C. | Predicting

- Explain that the word *gist* means the main point or general meaning of the reading.

- Ask volunteers to read the title, subheads, and opening paragraph aloud. Then have students predict the gist of the reading based on those three things.

- Note: Students will check their prediction later, in exercise **A** on page 14.

Exercise D. | Brainstorming

A word web is a visual way to organize important information. Explain that identifying key concepts and related vocabulary before they read will help students understand the important information in the reading.

TIP For exercise D, you may want to draw the chart on a large piece of paper and stick it on the wall. Then have students come up to the chart and write their words on it with marker pens.

 track 1-03 Ask students to read the article. Explain that the vocabulary definitions in the footnotes at the bottom of page 13 will help them understand the reading.

Overview of the Reading

The reading passage is adapted from Dan Buettner's book *Thrive: Finding Happiness the Blue Zones Way*. The passage:

– identifies six common factors that affect everyone's happiness.

– suggests that paying attention to these six factors will make you happier.

– indicates that all six factors are important.

– concludes that the place where you live is probably the most important factor.

For more information on the reading *Six Keys to Happiness*, see the Live Happier part of the Blue Zones website: http://www.bluezones.com/live-happier/

There's also a happiness survey that your students may like to try: http://apps.bluezones.com/happiness/

Vocabulary Notes

takes the focus off (paragraph B) = takes attention away from

long-lasting (paragraph D) = things that last a long time

enrich (paragraph D) = improve; add value

eat right (paragraph E) = eat healthy food

do your best (paragraph E) = try as hard as you can

moai (paragraph E) = a social network of close friends common in Okinawa

Understanding the Reading
(page 14)

Exercise A. | Understanding the Gist

Check students' predictions in exercise **C** on page 11.

Answer Key

The answer is c. The general idea or gist of the article—indicated in the title, subheads, and opening paragraph—is that there are some basic changes you can make to become happier. Item b is not correct because the article states that all factors are important, and item c is a specific conclusion in the last paragraph, not the general idea or gist.

Exercise B. | Identifying Main Ideas

- Explain that each sentence refers to one paragraph of the reading.
- Ask students how they usually go about finding the main idea.
- Draw attention to the **Strategy** box. Look back at the opening paragraph of the reading and identify where the main idea is (the second sentence).
- Do the first item as an example if necessary. Then allow students time to work individually.
- Compare answers as a class.

Answer Key

Self a. **Home** b. **Financial Life** a. **Social Life** a. **Workplace** a. **Community** a.

Exercise C. | Identifying Key Details

- Explain that key details give examples or more information about main ideas in a reading.
- Do the first item as an example if necessary.
- Ask students to work individually at first. Then compare answers in pairs.

Answer Key

1. . . . it takes the focus off your own problems.
   Or: . . . it makes you feel grateful for what you have.
2. . . . in difficult times.
3. . . . financial equality.

Exercise D. | Personalizing

- Explain that applying ideas from a reading to their own lives can help students understand and remember new information. You can share your own responses first to give students ideas if needed.
- When students finish writing their ideas, have them share notes with a partner, in small groups, or as a class. Share your ideas if you haven't done so previously.

Exercise E. | Critical Thinking: Synthesizing

Encourage students to look back at the readings to remember the main points.

Possible answers: 1. self (sense of purpose), social life (friends), community (live near people who have the same level of income as you)

2. love, spiritual life, a clean and beautiful environment

Exploring Written English

45 mins

(page 15)

Exercise A. | Brainstorming

- Draw attention to the **Strategy** box.
- Explain that brainstorming is a useful first step to gathering ideas before writing.
- Ask students to work in pairs to write words or phrases in their books or on a piece of paper. Walk around the class as students work and help them with ideas if needed.

Exercise B. | Journal Writing

- Explain that journal writing is another strategy for generating ideas. The writing style is more personal and informal, and students should not worry about grammatical errors. The important thing is to write an interesting personal response to the question.
- Allow time for students to work individually. Walk around as students write and offer help or suggestions as needed.

Exercise C. | Language for Writing

- Go over the information in the box.
- Have students complete the sentences.

Answer Key

1. has 2. see 3. are 4. don't 5. don't

IDEAS FOR... **Presenting Grammar**

For exercise **C,** write additional examples on the board of sentences with errors for students to correct. Students can also write their sentences from exercise **D** on the board for classmates to check.

Exercise D. | Applying

- Monitor students as they work and help them with ideas if needed.
- Have students share their sentences with a partner or the class.

Writing Skill: Writing a Topic Sentence

- Go over the information in the box. Point out how writing a topic sentence relates to the skill of finding the main idea of the paragraph in a reading—that is, the topic sentence introduces the main idea of the paragraph. If the topic sentence is strong and is stated clearly, it should be easy for readers to identify.

- Compare the strong and weak examples of topic sentences and ask students to identify the differences.

Exercise E. | Identifying Topic Sentences

- Advise students to read through each paragraph first before attempting to find the topic sentence.
- Check the answers as a class. Discuss how each detail in the paragraph relates to the main idea.

Answer Key

The topic sentence in paragraph 2 is stronger than the others.
1. Family members provide support to each other during difficult times. (Sentences 3 and 4 do not specifically mention difficult times.)
2. Studies have shown that laughter may be an important factor for our happiness, and people who laugh a lot are happier. (Sentence 1 presents an argument. Sentences 2, 3, and 4 support the argument.)
3. Our work can increase our happiness. (The first two sentences can be combined.)

Exercise F.

- Walk around and monitor students as they work. Provide assistance as needed.
- Ask volunteers to read their revised topic sentences.

Answer Key

1. In Mexico, getting support from family members is an important factor in being happy.
2. Because we spend most of our daily lives at work, doing a job that we enjoy can increase our happiness.

Writing Task: Drafting

(page 17)

Exercise A. | Planning

- Go over the steps in this exercise.
- Remind students that complete sentences are not necessary at this stage, and that it is more important to focus on their ideas than on grammar or spelling.
- Point out that the details need to support the topic sentence. The topic sentence and the details have to work together in the paragraph.
- Walk around and monitor students as they work. Provide assistance as needed.

- Ask three or four volunteers to read their topic sentence and discuss them as a class.

Exercise B. | Draft 1

Walk around and monitor students as they work. Provide assistance as needed.

TIP When giving students feedback on exercise B, make sure to focus on the content of the ideas, not on grammar or spelling. The important thing at this stage is for students to develop appropriate and interesting ideas in response to the question.

Writing Task: Revising
(page 18)

Exercise C. | Analyzing

- Writing usually requires two or more drafts. Point out that in this activity, students will compare two drafts of a paragraph to see how revising can improve the first draft. Doing this activity will help students to revise their own writing.
- Ask students to work in pairs to discuss the question.
- Ask volunteers to explain the reasons for their choice.
- Draw attention to the **CT Focus** box. Ask students to explain whether *passionate* is a good or bad feeling using the context. (It is a good feeling because of the context clue *great* in the sentence before: *I have a great job.*) Can they guess what *a raise* means? (The sentence before *a raise* in paragraph b says *I don't make a lot of money*, which can help students guess that ask for *a raise* means ask for *more money or a higher salary* at work.)

Answer Key

Paragraph b is the first draft, paragraph a is the revision. The topic sentence in paragraph a refers to *most things in my life*, not just work, and then gives examples. Paragraph b contains sentences that do not relate to the main idea: *I don't make a lot of money, so sometimes I have to do extra work on the weekends. I want to ask for a raise at work.*

Exercise D. | Analyzing

- Ask students to work in pairs to discuss their answers.
- Go over the answers together as a class.

Answer Key

	a	b
1.	Y	N
2.	Y	N
3.	Y	Y
4.	N	Y
5.	Y	Y

Exercise E. | Revising

- Explain that asking the questions in exercise **D** will help students to improve their own writing.
- Walk around and monitor students as they work. Provide assistance as needed.

Writing Task: Editing
(page 19)

TIP Some students may be surprised that a paragraph might need several revisions. Explain that even good writers often do several drafts of an essay. The first or second drafts usually focus on getting the ideas well organized and clearly presented. The final drafts usually focus on details such as spelling and punctuation.

Exercise F. | Peer Evaluation

- Explain that peer evaluation is a good way to get individualized feedback on your writing. All writers need to get feedback on their writing in order to improve.
- Discuss the four steps in the evaluation process to make sure students understand what they are to do.
- The purpose of this peer evaluation is to see if each student's partner, or peer, can identify the main ideas and details that he/she intended in the first draft.

Exercise G. | Draft 2

Monitor students as they work, and provide assistance as needed.

Exercise H. | Editing Practice

- The purpose of this exercise is to give students additional practice in editing for grammar to prepare them to do the **Editing Checklist** for their second draft. Focusing on grammar and punctuation at this stage prepares students to write their final draft.
- Go over the information in the box, and then have students edit the five sentences.
- Check the answers by asking students to read out the correct sentences and explain the errors.

Answer Key

1. I enjoy the work I do because it's very challenging, but I **don't** like my boss or my coworkers.
2. My coworkers are supportive, friendly, and fun, and I **enjoy** spending time with them after work.
3. It's important to me to spend time with my family members when I can, but it's difficult because they don't **live** close to me.
4. Although my house is not big and fancy, my neighborhood **is** safe and beautiful.
5. My friends and I **exercise** together every day to stay healthy, and that contributes to our happiness.

Writing Task: Editing *(page 20)*

Exercise I. | Editing Checklist

- Read the sentences in the editing checklist.
- Allow time for students to read and edit their work.
- Ask students for some examples of each type of error.

Exercise J. | Final Draft

Have students complete their third draft, and then collect their work.

> **TIP** You can use students' paragraphs to collect (anonymous) examples of good topic sentences and common errors for the next class.

Unit Quiz

- Students can work in groups to answer the questions.
- Encourage students to refer back of the relevant pages of the unit to find the answers.
- To do the quiz as a competition, you can have students work in teams.

Answer Key

1. Costa Rica
2. standard
3. Singapore
4. Mexico
5. main idea
6. grateful
7. close, happy friend
8. community

IDEAS FOR... Vocabulary Review

Ask students to create their own quiz based on vocabulary in this unit. Have students work in groups. Assign one reading or the video lesson to each group. Then have groups exchange quizzes and answer the questions without looking at the book. Alternatively, have each group select vocabulary items from anywhere in the unit.

IDEAS FOR... Journal Writing

At the end of this unit, ask students to write about a) their own interpretations of the word *happiness;* b) what advice they would give someone on how to be happy; or c) what advice they would give on how to live a long life.

IDEAS FOR... Further Research

Ask students to find out about other research into happiness or longevity and to write a short report about what they find out. They can present their reports to the class in the next lesson.

Possible website:

http://www.bluezones.com/

Big Ideas

Academic Track
Interdisciplinary

Academic Pathways:
Lesson A: Understanding a biographical text
Identifying supporting ideas
Lesson B: Ranking ideas in order of priority
Lesson C: Supporting the main idea and giving details
Writing a descriptive paragraph

Unit Theme

How do people come up with new inventions? Is it luck or hard work or a combination of the two?

Nanotechnology is the study of extremely tiny particles—that is, matter or materials on an atomic and molecular scale. Nanotechnology deals with anything measuring between 1 and 100 nanometers. (A nanometer [nm] is one-billionth of a meter.) Scientists are currently experimenting with substances at the nanoscale to learn about their properties and how to use them. For example, engineers are trying to use nano-size wires to create smaller, more powerful microprocessors and doctors are looking for ways to use nanoparticles in medical applications.

Unit 2 explores the topic of scientific breakthroughs as it relates to:

– windmills
– solar stoves
– seat belts
– innovations that help developing countries

Think and Discuss (page 21)

- Ask students how they think the nanotechnology in the photo might work? Can they think of any other examples? (Possible answer: The tiny silica balls attack and kill cancer cells in the human body without damaging healthy cells or tissue, or creating side effects as in chemotherapy.)

- Discuss question 1 as a class. Make a list of famous inventors and their inventions on the board. Explain that some of the readings in this unit will be about famous inventions.

- Discuss question 2. Ask students what inventions they have with them right now and which ones they have at home. Make a class list.

Exploring the Theme

(pages 22–23)

The opening spread features photographs of three important inventions: the airplane, the telephone, and the combustion engine.

- Ask students to look at the pictures and say how these inventions changed the world.

- Have students read the text. Ask what is similar and different about these inventions.

- Read the list of inventions aloud and ask students to explain what each one does.

- Lead a class discussion about questions 1–3.

> **TIP** For question 1, have students work in groups and think of five additional inventions to add to the list. Then have the class compare lists and decide on the five most important inventions.

IDEAS FOR... Expansion

- Ask students to create a general knowledge quiz about inventions for homework. In class, have students work in pairs to take turns taking each other's quiz.
- Ask students to find out more about nanotechnology. Then have them work in groups to present their information.

Preparing to Read *(page 24)*

30 mins

WARM-UP

The Lesson A target vocabulary is introduced in a matching exercise.

- **Ask students what they know about life in Malawi. What problems do they think there are? (Possible answers: population growth, economic hardships, food and water shortages, extreme weather, etc.)**

- **Bring in a world map and identify the location of Malawi. What do students think the climate is like there? (Possible answer: The climate is subtropical, with a rainy season and a dry season.)**

Exercise A. | Building Vocabulary

- Ask students to read the definitions and try to guess the missing words.

- Direct students to look at the words in blue in the reading and try to match them with the definitions.

- Check the answers by asking volunteers to read out a sentence each.

- Draw students' attention to the **Word Link** box. Discuss the meanings of these words and ask for example sentences. Note that the base form of the verb may require some transformation when adding a suffix to make it a noun. For example, the verb *prevent* becomes *prevent**ion**; define* becomes *defin**ition**; create* becomes *crea**tion**,* etc.

- Suggest that students list words that form nouns with the suffix *-tion* in their vocabulary notebooks.

> **TIP** Encourage students to use context to guess the meanings of unfamiliar words before consulting a dictionary.

Answer Key

1. afford	6. creative
2. powered	7. eventually
3. efficient	8. prevention
4. electricity	9. equipment
5. solar power	10. diagram

Exercise B. | Using Vocabulary

- Allow time for students to work in pairs to discuss the questions.

- Invite volunteers to share their answers with the class. (Possible answers to question 3: geothermal power, hydropower, wind, etc.)

Exercise C. | Brainstorming

- Allow time for students to complete their answers individually and then compare answers in pairs.

- Ask for volunteers to give their answers and write them on the board.

- Discuss which energy sources for producing electricity are most common in your country. Lead a class discussion to compare the possible advantages and disadvantages of each source.

> **TIP** If pairs finish their lists early, ask them to rank the things according to which ones use the most electricity.

Exercise D. | Predicting

- Remind students that predicting is something you do before reading the passage. It helps you to anticipate what is in the text and makes it easier to understand new information.

- Ask students to describe the pictures and to read out the title and the subheads. Write some of the students' predictions on the board.

- Note: Students will check their predictions later, in exercise **A** on page 27.

track **1-04** Ask students to read the passage. Explain that the vocabulary definitions in the footnotes at the bottom of pages 25 and 26 will help them understand the reading.

IDEAS FOR... Expansion

Ask students to use the diagram to explain how a windmill works to pump water from underground.

Overview of the Reading

The passage is about a young man from Malawi who built his own windmills. He used the windmills to make electricity and pump water from underground. You can find out more about William Kamkwamba at: http://blogs.ngm.com/blog_central/2009/10/the-windmills-of-his-mind.html

You can search for a video of William talking about his windmill on: http://www.ted.com/

Understanding the Reading

(page 27)

Exercise A. | Understanding the Gist

Check students' predictions in exercise **D** on page 24. Did they correctly guess what the reading is about?

Answer Key

The correct answer is item 3. Although items 1 and 2 are true, they are both supporting ideas—not the main idea of the passage.

Vocabulary Notes

severe (paragraph A) = very bad
starve (paragraph A) = not have any food
confident (paragraph C) = sure that something will happen in the way you want it to
trust yourself (paragraph E) = believe you can succeed

Exercise B. | Identifying Key Details

- Allow time for students to go back to the reading and write the answers.
- Monitor students while they are working and identify which sentences cause the most difficulty.
- Check the answers by asking questions about each sentence. For example, *Why did life become very challenging for William's family?*
- Ask students to elaborate on each answer by asking questions. For example, *Can you tell me more about why the drought caused so much difficulty?* (Because most people in Malawi don't have any water supply.)

Answer Key

1. there was a severe drought
2. *Using Energy*
3. laughed at him
4. someone else had built one
5. get power for their cell phones
6. bring water up from underground

Exercise C. | Critical Thinking: Making Connections

- Explain that this kind of graphic organizer can help to clarify and organize ideas from the reading. It's a good way to take notes and review important information.
- Ask students to work in pairs to complete the chart. Draw the chart on the board.
- Ask volunteers to write their answers in the chart. Ask the others in the class if they agree or disagree.

Answer Key

		He didn't have the parts and equipment.			
He went to the library.	He used the diagrams.			He used the windmill to pump water.	He taught other people to build windmills.

Exercise D. | Personalizing

- Allow time for students to complete their answers individually and then compare their answers in pairs or small groups.
- Ask students to write a paragraph in their journals about their answer to question 1.

TIP For question 2 of exercise D, assign a different invention to each pair so that more inventions are covered.

IDEAS FOR... Checking Comprehension

Write this instruction on the board: *Make a list of adjectives to describe William's personality. Support your opinions with details from the reading.*
Alternatively, write this list of adjectives on the board and have students find the supporting details.
(Possible adjectives describing William; supporting ideas are in parentheses.)

curious (He went to the library.)
resourceful (He went to the junkyards to find parts.)
creative (He found alternative parts for his windmill.)
persistent (He didn't give up.)
confident (He wasn't discouraged by others' opinions.)
hardworking/determined (He kept trying to improve his windmill.)
ambitious (He went back to school.)
generous (He used his ideas to help others in his village and his country.)

IDEAS FOR... Expansion

Have students work in pairs to role-play an interview between a newspaper reporter and William. Then have them switch roles and create an interview between the reporter and someone from William's village.

Developing Reading Skills

45 mins

(page 28)

Reading Skill: Identifying Supporting Ideas

- Review the difference between the main idea and supporting ideas.
- Explain to students that being able to identify supporting ideas will help them to read more rapidly and more effectively.
- Go over the first three lines of the paragraph.
- Ask a different student to read out each section (black, green, blue, and purple) of the paragraph. Tell students to cover the last three lines in the box and to match the sections to their functions: describe, give reasons, give examples.
- Check answers by having students uncover the last lines in the box.

> **TIP** Another way to use the material in the box is to write the sentences on different pieces of paper. Then ask students to match them with their function in the paragraph and put them in the best order.

Exercise A. | Analyzing

track 1-05

- Ask students to look at the picture and say what they know about seat belts. Why are they necessary? How is their design important to their effectiveness?
- Allow time for students to write their answers individually. (Explain that they should summarize using short phrases, not by copying the sentences.)
- Ask students which of the supporting details describe, give reasons, or give examples.

Answer Key

Main idea: a new type of seat belt has saved a lot of lives.
Supporting detail 1: old seat belts were buckled across the stomach
Supporting detail 2: they caused injuries
Supporting detail 3: new design holds upper and lower body in place

Exercise B. | Identifying Supporting Details

- Allow time for students to look back at the reading on pages 25–26 and find the answers.
- Allow time for students to write their ideas individually.

Answer Key

Possible answers:
a reason (Paragraph B): He wanted to continue his education.
an example (Paragraph D): First, the windmill powered only one light bulb.
describes (Paragraph D): This one brought water up from underground.

IDEAS FOR... **Multi-level Classes**

Higher-level students may want to try and find several examples of each type of supporting idea in the reading.

Viewing: Solar Cooking
(page 29)

Overview of the Video

This video is about a stove that uses energy from the sun to cook food. It is better for the environment as it does not produce pollution. People do not have to gather wood for fires. It can help to improve the lives of people in developing countries around the world.

Before Viewing

Exercise A. | Matching

- Ask students to look at the picture and suggest ways that solar cooking might work.
- Ask students to work individually or in pairs to match the words.
- Compare answers as a class and ask students to suggest other sentences using these words.

Answer Key

1. pollution	**4.** purify
2. absorb	**5.** alternative
3. developing world	**6.** fuel

Exercise B. | Brainstorming

- Remind students that brainstorming means thinking of as many ideas as possible, writing them all down, and then evaluating them.
- Allow time for students to work in pairs. Then ask volunteers to write their answers on the board. (Possible answers: can cause air pollution, people can't always find wood, people have to travel far to find wood, can set other things on fire, dangerous for people to breathe in smoke)

While Viewing

Exercises A and B.

- Ask students to read the questions in exercise **B**.
- Play the video while students take notes.

Answer Key

1. They direct sunshine onto a dark pot that then absorbs the sunshine and changes the light energy to heat energy.

2. People can cook with them; solar stoves can also purify water. People in poor areas of the world who cannot afford a stove or who usually use wood to cook can benefit from them.

3. It costs five dollars and can last two years.

After Viewing

Exercise A.

- Allow a few minutes for pairs to discuss and compare answers.
- Play the video again and check answers.

Exercise B. | Critical Thinking: Synthesizing

- Have students work in pairs, referring back to the reading as necessary, and then discuss the answers as a class.
- Have volunteers circle the things on the board that are mentioned in the video.

Answer Key

Possible answers:
They are both creative ways to improve people's lives with very few resources. They help reduce air pollution.

30 mins

Preparing to Read *(pages 30–31)*

WARM-UP

The Lesson B target vocabulary is presented in sentences about creative designs and inventions. Ask students to name one invention that they have heard about recently in the news.

Exercise A. | Building Vocabulary

- Do the first item together with the class as an example.
- Remind students to note the part of speech when they record new words in their vocabulary notebooks.
- Draw students' attention to the **Word Link** box. Remind students that learning prefixes and suffixes can help expand their vocabulary. Ask students to find five more examples of words that end in *–able*. (Possible answers: *admirable, avoidable, acceptable, honorable, predictable*)

Answer Key

1. noun; something such as a box or bottle that is used to hold things in
2. verb; notice, discover, or find
3. verb; give advantages to, have a good effect on
4. verb; show or demonstrate
5. noun; new things or new methods of doing something
6. noun; an object that has been invented for a particular purpose
7. adjective; always available, can be renewed
8. verb; put somewhere and leave it there until it is needed
9. noun; way of working, organizing, or doing something that follows a plan or set of rules
10. adjective; useful and helpful

Exercise B. | Using Vocabulary

- Give an example of your own for the first item if necessary.
- Allow time for students to complete the answers individually and then compare answers in pairs.
- Ask volunteers to read out their sentences. Take notes on any common errors and give feedback.

> **TIP** For question 1 of exercise B, you may want to list students' answers on the board in different categories such as *health, technology, communication, transportation,* etc.

Exercise C. | Predicting

- Draw attention to the **Strategy** box and remind students of the importance of predicting before reading in detail.
- Ask volunteers to read the title, subheads, and opening paragraph aloud.

- Note: Students will check their predictions later, in exercise **A** on page 34.

> **IDEAS FOR...** Checking Comprehension
>
> What do these inventions all have in common? (Possible answers: They are useful, affordable, inexpensive to produce, and can greatly benefit people's lives. They were all invented to help people in developing countries.)

track **1-06**

Ask students to read the article. Explain that the vocabulary definitions in the footnotes at the bottom of pages 32–33 will help them understand the reading.

Overview of the Reading

The reading passage is about five inventions that can help improve people's lives around the world. They are inexpensive to produce, yet can have a huge impact. The five inventions are:

- an infant warmer to keep low-birthweight babies warm and help them survive
- a container that allows people to carry water over long distances
- a clay cooler to keep food fresh
- a health detector to see if people are sick
- a solar Wi-Fi light that uses energy from the sun to power streetlamps and Internet access.

For more information about the infant warmer, see: http://embraceglobal.org/

For more information about the Q drum, see: http://www.qdrum.co.za/

The idea of the Q Drum was developed in response to the needs of rural people in southern Africa, where women had to carry heavy loads of water over long distances to their families. Women often suffered serious back, neck, and spine injuries from carrying heavy loads on their heads. The Q Drum reduces the load and also increases the volume by rolling water in a cylindrical vessel.

For more information about Hayat Sindi, see: http://www.nationalgeographic.com/explorers/bios/hayat-sindi/

More information about the health detector:
The device is produced by etching micro-channels and wells onto a small square of paper and pre-filling the wells with chemicals. To perform a test, a drop of saliva, urine, or blood is placed on the paper. The fluid travels through the channels, and a chemical reaction occurs that causes the spot to change color. Results show up in less than a minute and can be easily read using a color scale that is provided with the device.

Understanding the Reading
(page 34)

Vocabulary Notes

birthweight (paragraph B) = how much a baby weighs when it is born
embrace (paragraph B) = hug
trend (paragraph B) = tendency
localized (paragraph B) = in a nearby area
potential (paragraph B) = possibility
impact (paragraph B) = effect
portable (paragraph D) = can be carried
Wi-Fi (paragraph F) = can connect to the Internet wirelessly

Exercise A. | Understanding the Gist

Check students' predictions in exercise **C** on page 31.

Answer Key

Infant Warmer: to keep low-birthweight babies warm
Water Container: to make it easier to carry clean water over long distances
Portable Clay Cooker: to store food without electricity
Health Detector: to detect health problems
Solar Wi-Fi Light: to power streetlamps at night and provide wireless Internet access

Exercise B. | Identifying Key Details

- Allow time for student to work in pairs.
- Compare answers as a class.

Answer Key

1. T 2. F 3. F 4. T 5. NG

Exercise C. | Identifying Supporting Ideas

- Explain or elicit that supporting ideas can describe, give reasons, and give examples.
- Do the first item as an example if necessary.
- Have students work individually and then compare answers in pairs.

Answer Key

1. Because they cannot keep their bodies warm.
2. 13 gallons of water.
3. Water evaporates from the sand and keeps the food cool.
4. To find out if they are sick.
5. They can have better street lighting and faster communication.

Exercise D. | Critical Thinking: Ranking and Justifying

- Draw students' attention to the **CT Focus** box. Explain the meaning of *ranking* (putting in order according to certain criteria) and *justifying* (explaining how each item met the criteria).
- Help students to establish their criteria for considering the importance of an invention. You may want to brainstorm possible criteria on the board—for example, affordable, saves lives, useful for everyday life, protects the environment.
- Have students work in pairs to decide their criteria and then rank the items.
- Invite pairs to present their decisions to the class, explaining their criteria as they do so.

Exercise E. | Critical Thinking: Synthesizing

- Allow time for students to discuss their answers in groups, referring back to the video page of the lesson and their notes.
- Discuss answers as a class.

Answer Key

Possible answers:
Differences: The clay cooler is made of clay; the solar cooker is made of cardboard.
Similarities: Both are cheap to make and use local resources.

Exploring Written English

45 mins

(page 35–36)

Exercise A.

- Go over the information in the box.
- Ask students to complete the sentences individually and then compare answers in pairs.
- Check the answers as a class. Ask volunteers to identify the irregular verbs.

Answer Key

1. didn't have
2. went
3. found
4. used, built
5. started, didn't believe
6. wasn't, was
7. was, made

Exercise B. | Applying

- Allow time for students to write their answers individually.
- Monitor students as they write and identify any problem areas.
- Give general feedback on common problems that you found.

Exercise C. | Brainstorming

- Have students work in pairs. You may want to set a target number of innovations, such as 12 or 20.

Exercise D. | Journal Writing

- Remind students that journal writing is a way of generating ideas without worrying about grammar or spelling.
- You may want to give some possible sentence starters if students are having difficulty. For example, *The biggest changes in people's lives have been caused by . . . because . . .* Or: *Some innovations such as . . . have had a huge impact on people's lives because . . .*

Writing Skill: Supporting the Main Idea and Giving Details

- Go over the information in the box.
- Remind students of the paragraph they analyzed on page 28, where they identified three different types of supporting details.

Exercise E. | Identifying Supporting Ideas

- Advise students to read through all the sentences first to get an overview before attempting to find the answers.
- Allow time for students to work individually. Walk around the class and offer help as needed.

- Students who finish early can compare answers in pairs.
- Check the answers as a class. Ask volunteers to say why sentences b and f are extra. (Possible answer: They don't give information or details about the main idea.)

Answer Key

Topic Sentence A: a, d, h
Topic Sentence B: c, e, g

Exercise F.

- Allow time for students to work individually.
- Walk around and monitor students' work. Provide assistance as needed.

Answer Key

About 900 million people need access to safe drinking water, and a simple invention may be the answer to this problem. The LifeStraw provides instant clean water, saving lives during disasters. Thousands of LifeStraws were donated to Haiti after the 2010 earthquake. Each straw purifies about 160 gallons of water.

The solar-powered MightyLight is a safe and clean source of lighting that can provide light to millions of people around the world. The MightyLight is safer and cleaner than traditional kerosene lamps. It's easy to carry, and you can hang it on a wall or place it on a tabletop. It also lasts longer—its LED technology is good for up to 30 years.

Writing Task: Drafting *(page 37)*

Exercise A. | Planning

- Go over the steps in this exercise.
- Remind students that complete sentences are not necessary at this stage and that it is more important to focus on their ideas than on grammar or spelling.
- Point out that the details need to support the topic sentence. The topic sentence and the details have to work together in the paragraph.
- Walk around and monitor students as they work. Provide assistance as needed.
- Select some good topic sentences and details and read them aloud without mentioning whose they are. Discuss them as a class.

Exercise B. | Draft 1

Walk around and monitor students as they work. Provide assistance as needed.

Writing Task: Revising *(page 38)*

Exercise C. | Analyzing

- Point out that in this activity, students will compare two drafts of a paragraph to see how revising can improve the first draft. Doing this activity will help students to revise their own writing.
- Ask students to work in pairs to discuss the question.
- Ask volunteers to explain the reasons for their choice.

Answer Key

Paragraph b is the first draft. Paragraph a is the revision.

Paragraph b contains the following superfluous information: The first real car factory opened in 1902. A horse can go up to 40 miles per hour, but it gets tired after just a few miles. If the horse goes more slowly, it can travel for a longer period of time without getting tired.

Exercise D. | Analyzing

- Do the first item together as an example. What is the main idea of the paragraph?
- Ask students to work in pairs to discuss their answers.
- Go over the answers as a class.

Answer Key

	a	b
1.	Y	N
2.	Y	N
3.	Y	N
4.	Y	N
5.	N	Y
6.	Y	Y

Exercise E. | Revising

- Explain that asking the questions in exercise **D** will help students to improve their own writing.
- Allow time for students to make revisions to their paragraphs based on their answers.

Writing Task: Editing *(pages 39–40)*

Exercise F. | Peer Evaluation

- Remind students that peer evaluation will help them understand what makes a paragraph clear and well organized.
- Go over the four steps in this exercise.
- The purpose of this exercise is to see if the reader can identify the main idea, supporting ideas, and details that the writer intended.

Exercise G. | Draft 2

- Allow time for students to work on their second draft.
- Monitor students as they work and provide assistance as needed.

Exercise H. | Editing Practice

- Explain the importance of editing in good writing.
- Go over the information in the box.
- Allow time for students to read the sentences.
- Check the answers by asking students to read out the correct sentences and explain the errors.

Answer Key

1. The people in William Kamkwamba's village **weren't** confident about William's plan.
2. When they were young, the Wright brothers **had** a flying toy.
3. Alexander Graham Bell **made** the first telephone.
4. The first car didn't **go** very fast.
5. Ts'ai Lun invented paper in the first century AD, but paper **wasn't** widely available until many years later.

Exercise I. | Editing Checklist

- Read the sentences in the editing checklist.
- Allow time for students to read and edit their work.
- When students finish editing their work, ask for some examples of each type of error in the list.

Exercise J. | Final Draft

Have students complete their third draft, and then collect their work.

TIP **You may want to suggest that students keep copies of their drafts in a portfolio so that they can see how their writing develops over the course of several drafts.**

Unit Quiz

- Students can work in groups to answer the questions.
- Encourage students to refer back to the relevant pages of the unit to find the answers.
- To do this quiz as a competition, you can have students work in teams.

Answer Key

1. important invention **2.** solar **3.** electricity, water **4.** describe, give reasons, give examples **5.** solar cooker, solar stove **6.** innovation **7.** postage stamp **8.** base form

IDEAS FOR... Vocabulary Review

Put students in groups of four or five to play a picture game with some of the key words and phrases from this unit. Write each word or phrase on an index card and give a set of cards to each group. Each student in turn will pick up a card and, without showing it to the others, draw a picture to represent the word. They must not say or write any words. The first person to guess the word gets a point. If groups finish early, ask them to choose another word or phrase from this unit.

Key words and phrases:

air pollution
communication system
fuel shortage
health detector
junkyard
malaria prevention
portable cooler
renewable energy
seat belt
solar power
water container
windmill

IDEAS FOR... Journal Writing

At the end of this unit, ask students to write about a) their favorite innovation from this unit; b) advice they would give to someone who wants to be an inventor; or c) innovations they predict will be made in the next 10 years.

IDEAS FOR... Further Research

Ask students to find out about other innovations in science or technology and to write a short report about what they find out. They can present their report in the next class.

Possible Ideas:

Purifying Straw

Some 900 million people lack access to safe drinking water. Sipping through the LifeStraw filters surface water on-site, reducing the transmission of bacteria and viruses.

Sugarcane Charcoal

Briquettes made from crushed sugarcane stalks make use of an abundant local resource, and they burn more cleanly.

Affordable Laptops

The one laptop per child project aims to educate children in remote parts of the world. Governments purchase the computers, each equipped with Wi-Fi "rabbit-ears" and e-book mode, for schools.

Connected Lives

Academic Track
Anthropology/Sociology

Academic Pathways:
Lesson A: Skimming for gist
                  Making inferences
Lesson B: Reading a magazine article
Lesson C: Writing a concluding sentence
                  Writing an opinion paragraph

Unit Theme

How do people communicate via the Internet? How has it changed the way we communicate?
   The Internet is a global system of interconnected computer networks that connects billions of users worldwide. The Internet has enabled new forms of human communication through instant messaging, Internet forums, and social networking.

Unit 3 explores the topic of human communication as it relates to:

– new media on the Internet
– tradition and modernity in Lamu

– a new idea for an Internet start-up
– reading news and sharing music online

Think and Discuss (page 41)

- Ask students to describe the picture. Point out the caption in the lower-left corner. Are there similar Wi-Fi cafes where they live? Where do people typically gather to use the Internet?

- Discuss question 1 as a class. Make a list of ideas on the board. (Possible answers: email, social networking sites, Skype, texting, blogs, virtual worlds)

- Discuss question 2. Ask students to describe their own experiences with learning through the Internet. (Possible answers: videos and podcasts of lectures and lessons, research, distance learning)

- Explain that some of the readings in this unit will be about ways to communicate and learn via the Internet.

TIP   For question 2, divide the class into groups and have each group create a list of the advantages and disadvantages of learning via the Internet.

Exploring the Theme
(pages 42–43)

The opening spread features a map showing the density of IP addresses around the world and a graphic showing the number of visitors to various social networking sites in 2009.

- Ask students to look at the map and read the text. Discuss questions A1 and A2.

- Discuss questions B1 and B2 with the class.

Note: An Internet Protocol address (IP address) is a numerical label assigned to each device (e.g., computer, printer) participating in a computer network that uses the Internet for communication.

Answer Key

A1. They show the number of websites in that area.
A2. Japan, Europe, and North America are the most connected. South and East Asia, Latin America, and the Middle East had the biggest rise in Internet use. (Answers will vary.)
B1. The graphic shows which social networking sites are most popular and which countries use them most.
B2. Answers will vary.

TIP   For question B2, divide the class into groups and have each group create a list of the advantages and disadvantages of social networking sites.

IDEAS FOR... Expansion

Ask students to find out more about opportunities to learn on the Internet in their chosen field. Then ask them to summarize what they found out in the next class.

30 mins

Preparing to Read *(page 44)*

WARM-UP

The Lesson A target vocabulary is introduced in a matching exercise.

Ask students to suggest one way in which the Internet has changed the way we communicate. Find out how many students in the class have a website and/or a blog and have watched or posted a video on YouTube.

Exercise A. | Building Vocabulary

- Ask students to read the words in blue, and check (✓) the words they know and underline the ones they aren't sure about. Then have them match the two parts of the sentences.
- Check the answers by asking volunteers to read out a sentence each.
- Point out the **Word Link** box. Ask volunteers to suggest sentences using each of these words and to add other words to this list. (Possible answers: *interconnected, intermediate, intersect, interview, intervention,* etc.)

Answer Key

1. d 2. a 3. e 4. b 5. g 6. i 7. f 8. c 9. j 10. h

Exercise B. | Using Vocabulary

- Allow time for students to work in pairs to discuss the questions.
- Invite volunteers to share their answers with the class.

Exercise C. | Brainstorming

- Point out that the Venn diagram is a useful way to organize information to show what is the same or different about two concepts.
- Allow time for students to complete their answers individually.
- Draw the diagram on the board. Ask students to volunteer answers and write them on the board.
- Lead a class discussion about the innovations that have had the most impact on the world.

 TIP If pairs finish their lists early, ask them to team up with another pair and compare answers.

Answer Key *(Answers will vary.)*

TV: one-way communication, fixed choices
Both: get news, hear music, watch movies, see and hear advertising
Internet: interactive, can post messages and talk to others, can shop online

Exercise D. | Predicting

- Draw attention to the reading **Strategy** box. Explain that students will scan the passage in order to find specific words.
- Set a time limit of two minutes for students to scan the text.
- Note: Students will check their prediction later, in exercise **A** on page 47.

Answer Key

Possible answers: relationships, communication, information, Internet, connections

 track 1-07 Ask students to read the passage. Remind students that the vocabulary definitions in the footnotes at the bottom of pages 45 and 46 will help them understand the reading.

IDEAS FOR...	Expansion

Give students more practice with scanning. For example, they could scan the text on page 42 for dates or for names of countries.

Overview of the Reading

The reading passage describes how new media are changing our society and our relationships. The point is made that the newest media of communication—which are on the Internet—are more interactive than television, giving everyone a voice. This new style of communication can provide opportunities for sharing and collaboration, making it a valuable educational tool; however, everyone—especially students—must be aware of the dangers of digital media and learn to use it wisely.

More information can be found here:
http://www.nationalgeographic.com/explorers/bios/michael-wesch/

Understanding the Reading
(page 47)

Exercise A. | Understanding the Gist

Check students' prediction(s) in exercise **D** on page 44. Did they guess the general idea correctly?

Answer Key

The correct answer is item a. Although the use of the Internet in the classroom (item b) is discussed in the passage, it isn't the general idea. The importance of websites as compared to other forms of media (item c) is neither stated nor implied in the passage.

Exercise B. | Identifying Key Details

- Allow time for students to write their answers individually and then compare answers in pairs.
- Monitor students while they are working and identify the sentences that cause difficulty.
- Check the answers by inviting volunteers to come up and write them on the board.

Answer Key

1. social networks and other interactive Internet sites such as YouTube
2. the way families interacted
3. that it is two-way (Internet users can interact with the sites and communicate with one another.)
4. by connecting people with information and connecting people with people
5. that it can give misleading information
6. an online role-playing game
7. find, analyze, and think critically about online information, as well as create their own

Exercise C. | Critical Thinking: Making Inferences

- Draw students' attention to the **CT Focus** box. Explain that making inferences is an important reading skill. Writers don't always state information directly—sometimes the reader has to infer, or guess, the implied meaning from the information that is given.
- Give an example from the caption on page 43: *Today, the Internet helps young Bhutanese, such as these college students, stay connected with the rest of the world.* Ask students what the reader can infer from this sentence. (Possible answer: People in Bhutan do not have much contact with the rest of the world.)
- Ask students to work in pairs to choose the correct inferences.

- Check the answers with the class, asking students to give reasons for their choices.

Answer Key   1. a 2. b 3. a

Exercise D. | Personalizing

When students finish writing their answers, discuss the questions as a class, comparing answers and opinions.

IDEAS FOR...   Checking Comprehension

For question 2 in exercise **D**, lead a class discussion on Wesch's views. Try to reach a consensus on what they are and write them on the board. For example:
- The Internet is changing our relationships.
- Everyone can have a voice on the Internet.
- The Web represents (is a reflection of) our thoughts and ideas.
- Educational methods should change to suit new types of media.
- Students need new skills to deal with new media.
- Developments in new media are both positive and negative.
- The Internet can help people learn to collaborate more.
- People do not yet fully understand how to use the potential of the Web.

IDEAS FOR...   Expansion

- Have students work in pairs to debate one of Wesch's views and argue for and against its validity.
- Ask students to choose one of Wesch's views and write a paragraph in their journals about it.

Developing Reading Skills

45 mins *(page 48)*

Reading Skill: Skimming for Gist

- Go over the information in the box. Ask a volunteer to explain the difference between skimming and scanning. (Possible answer: Skimming is looking over a text to get the general idea of what it's about; scanning is reading for specific details.)

- Ask students to paraphrase the information in their own words and to give some examples of texts they would skim in everyday life.

Exercise A. | Skimming

- Set a time limit of one minute for students to skim the text.

- Have students work in pairs and write down what they think is the main idea of the paragraph. Point out that you will check answers in exercise **B**.

Exercise B. | Skimming

track **1-08**

- Draw students' attention to the **CT Focus** box. The writer doesn't say how people got the news in the past (before online social networks)—we have to infer, or guess, this from the information that is given about the ways people get news stories these days. (Possible answer: The writer probably got news from print magazines and newspapers, as well as TV and radio programs.)

- Check the answer as a class. (Option: Play the audio as students read.)

Answer Key

Main idea: Online social networks are changing our lives in many ways.

IDEAS FOR... Multi-level Classes

Higher-level students may try to find other examples of inferences that can be drawn from the reading. For lower-level students, provide some questions that will help them to make inferences. For example, *How did people keep in touch with friends before the Internet? Was it easy to stay in touch with old friends?* (Possible inference: It wasn't as easy to stay in touch, and people didn't contact one another as often.)

Viewing Lamu: Tradition and Modernity *(page 49)*

Overview of the Video

This video is about the old town of Lamu in Kenya, Africa. Lamu's civilization is centuries old, but now some of its people are learning to adapt to modern technology, using the Internet to make connections with the world.

Vocabulary Notes

unique = unusual, the only one of its kind
World Heritage Site = place that is protected because of its historical importance
absorb = assimilate
sheik = head of a tribe or a Muslim religious leader
trader = someone who buys and sells goods
blend in = mix
uneasy = difficult, awkward
mosque = Muslim place of religious prayer

Before Viewing

Exercise A. | Matching

- Ask students to look at the title and suggest what the video might be about. Where do they think Lamu is located? (in Kenya, Africa) How would they describe the houses there? (The houses are very close together.)
- Ask students to work in pairs to discuss and write definitions of the words.
- Compare answers as a class.

Answer Key

1. *influence* = effect on what people do or on what happens
2. *economic* = concerned with the organization of the money, industry, and trade of a country, region, or society
3. *dynamic* = constantly changing
4. *retain* = keep
5. *features* = aspects, characteristics

Exercise B. | Brainstorming

- Remind students that brainstorming means thinking of as many ideas as possible, writing them all down, and then evaluating them.
- Ask volunteers to write their ideas on the board.

Answer Key

Possible answers:
For: They can learn about other countries. They can get ideas for improving their lives.
Against: They are afraid of change. They don't want to be influenced by Western cultures.

While Viewing

Exercises A and B.

- Ask students to read the questions in exercise **B**.
- Play the video while students take notes.
- Ask volunteers to come to the board to circle the items that are mentioned in the video.

Answer Key

1. to increase trade and improve the economy
2. starting an Internet cafe
3. He wants to modernize without losing their traditional culture.

After Viewing

Exercise A.

- Have students discuss and compare their answers.
- Play the video again and check the answers with the class.

Exercise B. | Critical Thinking: Synthesizing

- Allow time for students to work in pairs or small groups to discuss the questions.
- Ask volunteers to share their answers with the class.

Answer Key

They used trade routes to exchange goods and ideas.

Preparing to Read *(pages 50–51)*

30 mins

WARM-UP

The Lesson B target vocabulary is presented in an exercise that requires students to get meaning from context.

Ask students to look at the picture of the island and say what they would like or dislike about living there.

Exercise A. | Building Vocabulary

- Ask students to choose if they want to work individually or in pairs.

- Explain that the words in blue are the new vocabulary words and that students should choose which meaning is correct by looking at the context clues here and in the reading.

- Do the first item together with the class as an example. (The key words *commercials* and *ads* appear in the sentence; these are ways to deliver messages, or tell people about something.)

- Ask volunteers to read out their answer for each question.

- After checking the answer to question 3, draw students' attention to the **Word Link** box. Ask students to find three more examples of words that end in –al. (Possible answers: *financial, educational, social, medical*)

- After completing the answers, point out the **Word Partners** box. Explain that some words, such as *environmentally*, often occur with other words in speech and writing. Another example is in item 5: the word *positive* is often used with other words, as in *positive influence, positive reaction.* Remind students that learning word partners can help them expand their vocabulary.

Answer Key

1. b 2. a 3. b 4. a 5. a 6. b 7. b 8. b 9. b 10. a

IDEAS FOR... **Expansion**

Ask students to try to make a sentence using two or more of these words. The student who includes the most words in one correct, logical sentence is the winner. Remind them to record these new words in their vocabulary notebooks.

Exercise B. | Using Vocabulary

- Give an example of your own for the first item.

- Allow time for students to complete the answers individually and then compare answers in pairs.

- Ask volunteers to read out their sentences.

TIP For question 4 of exercise B, you may want to list answers on the board and encourage students to give each other tips on how to use the Internet as a research tool. You could also start a class list of websites that are helpful for research.

Exercise C. | Predicting

- Ask students to read the title and subheads and then skim the passage for the answer to the question.

- Have students skim the reading and try to find the answer to the question. Have them write it down.

- Note: Students will check their prediction later, in exercise **A** on page 54.

IDEAS FOR... **Checking Comprehension**

Ask these questions or write them on the board.

1. What motivated Ben and Mark to develop this idea? (They wanted to create an Internet start-up.)

2. What aspects of their idea are most innovative in your opinion? (Possible answers: They created an online community and called it a tribe. They made decisions about rules with discussions and online voting. Then they went to Fiji and worked with a tribe to develop their island.)

3. Why is Mark critical of people who spend most of their time posting messages and sharing music? (He thinks social networking sites can be used for much more.)

4. How do you think this idea benefits the global community? (Possible answer: It brings together people and cultures, and helps places become more modern—without losing traditional culture.)

5. Would you like to join this community? Why, or why not? What do you think you would enjoy most? (Answers will vary.)

Vocabulary Notes

remote (paragraph A) = far from places where most people live, and therefore difficult to get to
sharing music (paragraph B) = uploading and downloading music files online
newcomers (paragraph G) = people who have recently arrived

IDEAS FOR... Discussion

Discuss these questions or assign them as journal-writing tasks for homework.

1. What problems do you think might occur between local villagers and newcomers?
2. How do you think they would communicate with each other?
3. What do you think will happen once the lease expires and the global tribe members leave?

Ask students to read the article. Remind them that the vocabulary definitions in the footnotes at the bottom of page 52 will help them understand the reading.

Overview of the Reading

The reading passage describes a new idea for an Internet company called Tribewanted.com. Using social media, the founders began their first project—on a small island in Fiji—by gathering a group of people who wanted to help develop sustainable projects together with the local community. A new location is in Sierra Leone.

Understanding the Reading
(page 54)

Exercise A. | Understanding the Gist

Check students' predictions in exercise **C** on page 51.

Answer Key

The title is "Internet Island" because the idea for Tribewanted.com came from social networking websites. Also, Tui Mali advertised his island online, and the people who worked with the local tribe members were brought together by the Internet.

Exercise B. | Identifying Main Ideas

- Ask several students to give their ideas and write them on the board. As a class, choose the best one.
- Allow time for students to work individually and then compare answers in pairs.
- Check answers with the class.

Answer Key

1. Paragraph 1: Two men decided to build an environmentally friendly community and share it with the world.
2. Paragraph 2: James wanted to take advantage of the full potential of the Internet.
3. Paragraph 3: Thanks to the Internet, Tui Mali and James and Keene were in contact, and they made arrangements for Tribewanted to provide jobs and income to the island.
4. Paragraph 4: Tribewanted worked together with the tribe members to make improvements to the island.

Exercise C. | Identifying Key Details

- Point out the **Strategy** box.
- Ask students to work individually to match the type of information that belongs in each blank.
- Check answers with the class.

Answer Key

1. b, Mark James 2. d, Tribewanted 3. h, Vorovoro
4. g, $53,000 5. e, 2006 6. c, fresh fish from the ocean
7. f, modern 8. a, Sierra Leone

Exercise D. | Critical Thinking: Making Inferences

- Remind students that inferences are not directly stated, but are suggested by details in the reading.
- Allow time for students to work in pairs, and then to present and explain their answers.

Answer Key

Possible answers:
1. The people who join Tribewanted want to help the environment. (paragraph A: We will build an environmentally friendly community and share it with the world.)
2. Tribewanted members can learn how to work together with other cultures. (paragraph G: For several weeks after the newcomers arrived, they worked with the local tribe members. … As they worked together, they became friends.)
3. They will learn about other cultures and get new ideas. (paragraph H: Through the Internet, the tribe connected with almost a thousand people from all over the world. On the island, it brought together groups of people from very different cultures.)

Exploring Written English
(pages 55–56)

45 mins

Exercise A.

- Go over the information in the box.
- Give some contrasting examples of sentences using the present perfect and the simple past. For example, *I have written three emails today. I wrote three emails yesterday.*
- Have students complete the sentences individually and then compare answers in pairs.
- Invite volunteers to read out their answers. Elicit or explain which meaning of the present perfect each sentence uses.

Answer Key

1. have changed
2. has used
3. has met
4. have found

Exercise B.

- Allow time for students to write their answers individually.
- Monitor students as they write, and identify any problem areas.
- Give general feedback on common problems that you found.

Exercise C. | Brainstorming

- Allow time for students to work in pairs to think of as many ideas as they can.
- Ask volunteers to call out their answers.

Exercise D. | Journal Writing

- Explain that this task will help students develop ideas for their writing in the next part of the lesson.
- Allow time for students to work individually.
- Walk around as students write, and offer help or suggestions as needed. Encourage students to use the new vocabulary and grammar from this unit.

Writing Skill: Writing a Concluding Sentence

- Go over the information in the box. Point out that a concluding sentence has one of several purposes, but the main purpose is to tie the paragraph together.
- Write the four sentence types on the board: *Q, P, O,* and *R.*
- Give an example of each one. Ask students to identify each type.

Examples: (Q) *Are books going to become obsolete?* (P) *Books will eventually disappear.* (O) *I believe that print resources are more reliable than Web sources.* (R) *These are some of the ways the Internet has changed the way we communicate.*

Exercise E. | Critical Thinking: Analyzing

- Advise students to read through all the sentences first to get an overview before attempting to find the answers.
- Allow time for students to work individually and then compare answers in pairs.
- Invite volunteers to write their answers on the board.

Answer Key   1. R 2. Q 3. P 4. O 5. P

Exercise F.

- Allow time for students to work individually.
- Walk around and monitor students' work. Provide assistance as needed.

Answer Key

Possible answers:
1. It is possible that although people spend more time socializing, they will not feel as happy as they did when they spent more time with friends and family in person.
2. To summarize, reading the news online has many advantages over getting the news from a newspaper or on TV.

Writing Task: Drafting *(page 57)*

Exercise A. | Planning

- Go over the steps in this exercise.
- Remind students that complete sentences are not necessary at this stage and that it is more important to focus on their ideas than on grammar or spelling.
- Point out that the topic sentence needs to state the main idea, the supporting ideas and details need to support the main idea, and the concluding sentence needs to tie the paragraph together.
- Walk around and monitor students' work. Provide assistance as needed.

Exercise B. | Draft 1

- Point out the **Strategy** box. Remind students that when they give an opinion, they should support it with reasons and details.

- Walk around and monitor students' work. Provide assistance as needed.

> **TIP** If higher-level students finish early, ask them to help lower-level students with developing and expressing their ideas.

Writing Task: Revising
(page 58)

Exercise C. | Analyzing

- Ask students what they can tell you about music sharing.

- Draw attention to the **CT Focus**. Ask students to think about the questions as they read. (Possible answers: The person probably uses the Internet a lot; he or she seems to be generally honest.)

- Point out that in this activity, students will compare two drafts of a paragraph to see how revising the first draft can improve it. Doing this activity will help students to revise their own writing.

- Have students work in pairs to discuss the questions.

- Ask volunteers to explain the reasons for their choice.

Exercise D. | Analyzing

- Do the first item together as an example. What is the main idea of the paragraph?

- Ask students to work in pairs to discuss their answers.

- Go over the answers together as a class.

Exercise E. | Revising

- Explain that asking the questions in exercise **D** will help students to improve their own writing.

- Walk around and monitor students as they work. Provide assistance as needed.

> **TIP** After monitoring students' work, you may want to list on the board some of the unit vocabulary or other extra vocabulary that you feel might be valuable for reference.

Exercise F. | Peer Evaluation

- Go over the four steps in this exercise to make sure students know what to do.

- Explain that peer evaluation will help students to see their paragraph from the reader's point of view.

- Remind students that it is important to be supportive and encouraging when giving feedback to their partner.

Exercise G. | Draft 2

Monitor students as they work, and provide assistance as needed.

Exercise H. | Editing Practice

- Go over the information in the box and allow time for students to read the sentences.

- Check the answers by asking students to read out the correct sentences and explain the errors.

Writing Task: Editing *(page 60)*

Exercise I. | Editing Checklist

- Read the sentences in the editing checklist.
- Allow time for students to read and edit their work.

Exercise J. | Final Draft

- Have students write their final draft, and then collect their work.

Unit Quiz

- Students can work in groups to answer the questions.
- Encourage students to refer back to the relevant pages of the unit to find the answers.
- To do the quiz as a competition, you can have students work in teams.

Answer Key

1. Internet access	**5.** social networking sites
2. TV	**6.** virtual
3. relationships, society	**7.** concluding sentence
4. skimming	**8.** have been

IDEAS FOR... Giving Corrective Feedback

You may want to use editing codes when you comment on students' work. This will help them to correct their own work and take more time to reread their final drafts. Make a list of these codes on the board so that students can copy them in their notebooks. They can refer to them when you give their work back to them. Some example codes:

SP (spelling)

GR (grammar)

T (tense)

WW (wrong word)

WF (word form)

SV (subject-verb agreement)

IDEAS FOR... Journal Writing

Ask students to write about a) their favorite way of communicating on the Internet; b) the difference between using print and Internet media; or c) how they think new media will develop in the future.

IDEAS FOR... Further Research

Ask students to find out about recent digital developments and to write a short report about what they find out. They can present their reports to the class in the next lesson.

Deep Trouble

Academic Track
Interdisciplinary

Academic Pathways:

Lesson A: Interpreting visual information
Examining problems and solutions
Lesson B: Understanding graphic information
Reading an interview
Lesson C: Explaining a chart or graph

Unit Theme

How much do we know about the oceans on our planet? How are our lives affected by oceans, and what impact do we have on ocean life?

Unit 4 explores the topic of oceans and seas as it relates to:

– overfishing of the world's oceans
– saving bluefin tuna

– how we can help to protect fish species
– farming of Atlantic salmon

Think and Discuss *(page 61)*

- Ask students to describe the picture. How do they think the diver feels? Ask how they feel about the ocean. (Possible answers: relaxed, afraid, calm, anxious) Ask if anyone in the class has gone diving? If so, where? How did it feel? What did they see? Ask students to explain why some people are fascinated by the ocean, want to explore it, play in it, or live near it.

- Discuss questions 1 and 2 as a class. Make a list of different kinds of seafood that are popular with your students.

Exploring the Theme

(pages 62–63)

The opening spread features a map showing the impact of human activity on the world's oceans, as well as a description of problems that exist in four of the world's seas.

- Before students answer questions 1–3, ask them to look at the pictures and guess what problems will be mentioned.

- Ask students to look at the map and read the text in the box. Discuss questions 1–2.

- Discuss question 3. Ask students to summarize the information about each place.

- Ask students questions about some of the vocabulary. For example, *What is a container ship? What are container ships used for? What is overfishing? Why do you think the temperature of the water increasing?* (Possible answer: It might be an effect of global warming.)

Answer Key

1. The colors show the impact of human activity. This refers to fishing, farming, manufacturing, and offshore gas and oil drilling.

2. The north Pacific and the north Atlantic especially around Europe, parts of Korea and Japan, the eastern coast of China, and parts of Southeast Asia.

3. In the Caribbean, fish species are disappearing because of pollution and overfishing. Rising water temperatures make it difficult for species to survive. In the North Sea, pollution and overfishing are causing areas where plants and fish don't have enough oxygen to live. Large rivers bring pollution into the East China Sea. Although the Coral Sea has less impact from human activity, the water is becoming warmer and acidic.

TIP For question 3, divide the class into four groups and have each group work on one of the places, listing the causes and effects of environmental damage.

IDEAS FOR... Expansion

Ask students to find out more about the world's oceans. What recent discoveries have been made? What mysteries are scientists still trying to solve?

Preparing to Read *(page 64)*

30 mins

WARM-UP

The Lesson A target vocabulary is presented as individual words in a box. Remind students that it is a good idea to familiarize themselves with vocabulary before seeing it in context.

Ask students what they know about the commercial fishing industry. Is it an important industry in their country? What problems might the industry create?

Exercise A. | Building Vocabulary

- Ask students to read the words in the box and circle the ones they know and underline the ones they aren't sure about.
- Have students find the words in the reading and guess their meanings.
- Check the answers by asking volunteers to read out a sentence each. Correct pronunciation if necessary.
- Draw students' attention to the **Word Partners** box. Ask students to suggest sentences using each of these phrases. For example, *The government wants to reduce spending on health and education.*
- Remind students to list word partners in their vocabulary notebooks.

Answer Key

1. reduce	6. ecosystem
2. survive	7. restore
3. diverse	8. estimate
4. species	9. population
5. quantity	10. stable

Exercise B. | Using Vocabulary

- Allow time for students to work in pairs to discuss the questions.
- Invite volunteers to share their answers with the class.

Answer Key

Possible answers:
1. Fish need the correct levels of food, temperature, water chemistry, and light to survive. People need food, water, and shelter.

2. We can reduce pollution by recycling more, reducing the number of cars on the road, using more wind and solar power, supporting local farmers, etc.

3. *Countries with the largest populations:* China, India, the U.S., Indonesia, Brazil; *Cities with the largest populations:* Tokyo, Jakarta, Mumbai, Delhi, Manila

---

TIP If pairs finish early, ask them to think of other questions using any of the target words in exercise A. When everyone has completed exercise B, have students ask the class their questions.

Exercise C. | Brainstorming

Have students work in groups and then share their ideas with the class.

Answer Key

Possible answers:
pollution, overfishing, rising water temperatures, damage caused by oil spills, nuclear accidents, "dead zones"

Exercise D. | Predicting

- Ask students to use the pictures, title, and subheads to predict what the reading is about. Write their prediction(s) on the board.
- Note: Students will check their prediction(s) later, in exercise **A** on page 67.

track **1-10**

Ask students to read the passage. Remind students that the vocabulary definitions at the bottom of pages 65 and 66 will help them understand the reading.

Overview of the Reading

The reading passage presents some of the causes and effects of overfishing in the world's oceans. It warns that many more fish could disappear and suggests some possible solutions to the problem.

Understanding the Reading
(page 67)

Exercise A. | Understanding the Gist

Check students' prediction(s) in exercise **D** on page 64. Did they guess the main idea correctly?

Answer Key

The correct answer is item b. Item a is false: There are fewer—not more—fish today. Although item c is factually correct, the passage focuses on overfishing—not on pollution.

Vocabulary Notes

limitless (paragraph A) = endless, without limit
trend (paragraph E) = change or development toward something new or different
largely (paragraph F) = mostly
prevent (paragraph F) = ensure that something doesn't happen

Exercise B. | Guessing Meaning from Context

- Allow time for students to go back to the reading and write their answers.
- Monitor students while they are working and identify which expressions cause difficulty.
- Check the answers as a class.

Answer Key

1. A, taking so many fish from the sea that species are disappearing
2. E, weeding out, or eliminating, the sick and weak fish
3. G, fish farming

Exercise C. | Identifying Main Ideas

- Allow time for students to go over the reading and write their answers. Remind them to support their answers with details from the passage.
- Ask volunteers to share their answers with the class. Encourage students to use complete sentences when giving their answers.

Answer Key

1. The main reason that big fish in the oceans are gone now is because of overfishing by the commercial fishing industry.
2. The commercial fishing industry can catch more fish than local fishermen because the commercial boats can use new technologies such as sonar to locate fish, and they can drag large nets along the ocean floor.
3. Large populations of little fish are a problem because ecosystems need predators to be stable.
4. If fishing continues at the current rate, most of the fish we catch now will disappear.

Exercise D. | Critical Thinking: Analyzing

- Draw students' attention to the **CT Focus** box. Read the information. Explain that asking these questions as they read will help students to critically evaluate the passage.
- Allow time for students to work in pairs and complete the chart.
- Draw the chart on the board and ask volunteers to come up and write their answers in each section. Ask the rest of the class if they agree.

Answer Key

Main Problem:
overfishing of the oceans by commercial fishing industry
Solutions:
1. catch fewer fish
2. develop aquaculture
3. stop eating fish that are in danger

Exercise E. | Critical Thinking: Evaluating Arguments

- Allow time for students to work in pairs to discuss their answers. (Possible answers should indicate that the writer provides enough supporting information by describing the causes and effects of the problems of overfishing. The writer also gives enough information to help the reader understand how the solution might work.)
- Discuss the questions as a class.

Exercise F. | Personalizing

- Ask students to work in pairs.
- When students finish their pair discussions, you may want to survey the class to see how students' eating habits might change after reading the passage.
- Suggest that students write an entry in their journal about their reactions to the information in the passage. Did they learn anything new that will affect their lives?

IDEAS FOR... Checking Comprehension

Ask students to compare fishing in the past and now. Draw a chart with two columns, *before* and *now*, on the board. Have students complete the chart in their notebooks.

Examples:

before: individual fishermen. small pole-and-line boats, smaller nets and manual fishing equipment

now: large fishing companies, large industrial trawlers, sonar, large nets, mechanical equipment

IDEAS FOR... Expansion

Have students work in pairs to debate for and against commercial fishing.

45 mins

Developing Reading Skills
(page 68)

Reading Skill: Interpreting Visual Information

- Go over the information in the box.

- Ask some basic comprehension questions about the graph. For example, *What does the x axis show?* (years) *What does the key tell you?* (which colors represent which oceans) *What does the title tell you?* (the main idea of the graph)

- Ask volunteers to summarize the information presented in the graph.

> **TIP** Ask students to find examples of other charts, graphs, maps, and other graphics in the previous units.

Exercise A. | Interpreting a Graph

After students have discussed the questions in pairs, compare the answers as a class.

Answer Key

1. It shows how much tuna was caught in three major oceans.
2. The dark blue color represents the Atlantic Ocean.
3. Approximately 1 million tonnes of tuna were caught in the Indian Ocean in 2000.

Exercise B. | Interpreting Maps

- Refer students to the maps on pages 62–63 and 66. Allow them time to answer the questions individually and then compare answers in pairs.

- Check answers with the class.

> **TIP** If students have difficulty answering these questions, prepare a list of easy questions for each map and hand them to each pair. They can take turns asking and answering the questions.

Answer Key

1. The map on page 66 shows which parts of the world's oceans were fished most intensively in the early 2000s. It uses a gradient color scale from low to high.
2. The map on pages 62–63 shows which parts of the world's oceans were most affected by various types of human activity—not just fishing.

Exercise C. | Critical Thinking: Synthesizing

After students have discussed the question in pairs, go over the answer as a class.

Answer Key

The Pacific Ocean because it is dark blue in the map on page 66 and has the largest quantity of catches on the graph (shown in light blue).

Viewing: Saving Bluefin Tuna *(page 69)*

Overview of the Video

This video is about a Japanese scientist who is trying to breed bluefin tuna in captivity. It is quite difficult to create conditions where this type of fish can breed, but he has been successful. After the fish are born, he returns them to the ocean. He hopes this will help to prevent the bluefin tuna from dying out.

Before Viewing

Exercise A. | Using a Dictionary

- Discuss the answers as a class.
- Ask students to predict how these words might be used in the video.

Answer Key

1. hatchlings 2. in captivity 3. breed 4. the wild

Exercise B. | Brainstorming

- Ask students to describe the pictures and read the captions.
- Make a list of students' ideas on the board. (Possible answers: to preserve biodiversity, to maintain the ecosystem of the ocean, as a food source)

While Viewing

Exercises A and B.

- Ask students to read the questions in exercises **A** and **B**.
- Play the video. Ask students to check their answers to the Brainstorming exercise in Before Viewing and to write short answers to questions 1–4 in exercise **B**.

Answer Key

1. by breeding them in captivity
2. It is difficult to create the right conditions for successful breeding.
3. It has declined to one-fifth of its former population in the Atlantic Ocean.
4. We have to reduce the number of fish we catch each year.

Vocabulary Notes

is on a mission = has a goal
extinct = without any living members, either in the world or in a particular place
significantly = greatly
relying on = depending on
dramatically = greatly
giants of the sea = reference to tuna, which are large and very important fish
eventually = after a period of time
die out = become extinct

After Viewing

Exercise A.

- After students have compared answers, check the answers as a class.
- Play the video again if necessary.

Exercise B. | Critical Thinking: Synthesizing

- Allow time for students to work in pairs, referring back to the reading as necessary.
- Ask volunteers to share their answers with the class.

Answer Key

Possible answers:
eat less fish, eat only small fish, stop eating fish

Preparing to Read *(pages 70–71)*

30 mins

WARM-UP

The Lesson B target vocabulary is presented in a sentence-completion exercise. Remind students that reading the whole sentence will help them figure out which word correctly completes it.

Exercise A. | Building Vocabulary

- Ask students to choose if they want to work individually or in pairs.

- Do the first item together with the class as an example if necessary.

- After checking the answer to question 4, draw students' attention to the **Word Link** box. Explain that learning the roots of words like this can help to expand vocabulary. Ask students to find more examples of words that start with *mini-*. (Possible answers: *mini-golf, miniskirt, mini-cam*)

- After checking the answers, point out the **Word Partnership** box. Remind students that using collocations like these can help to make their writing sound more confident and fluent.

- Ask students to find other forms for some of the words in exercise **A**. (Possible answers: *(adj.),* avoidable; *(n.)* decline; *(adj.)* reliable; *(n.)* information; *(adj.)* advisable.)

> **TIP** You may want to introduce this exercise by writing the target words on the board. Then read out the definitions in random order while students write their answers. Finally, students can check their answers in the book.

Answer Key

1. impact	6. essential
2. individual	7. rely on
3. avoid	8. informed
4. minimal	9. advice
5. declining	10. definitely

IDEAS FOR... Multi-level Classes

To make exercise **A** more challenging, suggest that students cover the target words and try to complete the sentences without looking at them. Then they can uncover the words to check their answers.

Exercise B. | Using Vocabulary

- Give an example of your own for the first item if necessary.

- Allow time for students to complete the answers individually and then compare answers in pairs.

- Ask one student from each pair to summarize their answers.

> **TIP** For question 3 of exercise B, hold a brief class discussion on which foods students avoid and why.

Exercise C. | Brainstorming

- Ask students to brainstorm ideas in pairs.

- Ask volunteers to come up and write their answers on the board. (Possible answers: stop eating fish with declining populations, clean up the beaches, volunteer to work with a conservation organization)

Exercise D. | Predicting

- Draw attention to the reading **Strategy** box. Point out that students have been using this strategy since Unit 1.

- Ask students to look at the titles and the visuals and write down their predictions.

- Note: Students will check their predictions later, after they read the passage.

 track 1-11

Ask students to read the article. Explain that the vocabulary definitions in the footnotes at the bottom of page 72 will help them understand the reading.

IDEAS FOR... Checking Comprehension

Make some false statements about the passage and ask students to correct you. Examples:

1. Seaver thinks we should stop eating fish. (He thinks we should stop eating the bigger fish of the sea.)

2. Mussels and oysters are not safe to eat. (Farmed mussels and oysters are all right to eat.)

3. Sturgeon and swordfish are herbivores. (Sturgeon and swordfish are top predators.)

4. Shrimp and clams are the lowest on the food chain. (Plants are the lowest on the food chain.)

Overview of the Reading

The reading passage is an interview with chef and conservationist Barton Seaver. His recommendations include:

– making better food choices when we eat

– eating farm-raised fish

– eating fish that are low on the food chain (such as small fish and shellfish)

– thinking more about our relationship with our environment

Barton Seaver is a National Geographic Fellow and Washington, D.C., chef. He has written and spoken widely on the topic of sustainable seafood.

You can find out more about him here: http://www.bartonseaver.org/

You can see a video of him talking about sustainable fishing by searching Barton Seaver under Speakers on this website: http://www.ted.com/

The oceans are facing threats from many sides—pollution, overfishing, and global warming. You can learn more about this topic here: http://ocean.nationalgeographic.com/ocean/protect/

You can find out more about overfishing here: http://ocean.nationalgeographic.com/ocean/critical-issues-overfishing/

Vocabulary Notes

well-managed fisheries = fish farms where fish are raised and fed in a way that maintains their numbers

the food chain = the sequence of who eats what in an ecosystem. For example, a shark eats a seal, the seal eats fish, the fish eats zooplankton, the zooplankton eats phytoplankton.

top predators = the largest carnivores

carnivores = creatures that eat meat

herbivores = creatures that eat plants

zooplankton = small organisms that drift in the water; some are too small to be seen, some are larger (like jellyfish)

phytoplankton = organisms in the uppermost layer of the ocean that process sunlight and carbon dioxide through photosynthesis to make energy

Understanding the Reading
(page 74)

Exercise A. | Understanding the Gist

- Check students' predictions in exercise **D** on page 71.
- Have students choose their answer individually and then compare answers in pairs.

Answer Key

The answer is item c. Seaver's main message is that people's food choices can help improve the oceans' health. Item a is not correct because he does not recommend that we stop eating seafood—only that we stop eating species that have been overfished and that are valuable to the environment. Item b is incorrect because the main theme of the article is seafood.

Exercise B. | Identifying Purpose

- The purpose of this exercise is to help students understand how graphics convey information visually.
- Check answers as a class and have students give reasons for their choices.

Answer Key   1. b 2. a

Exercise C. | Identifying Key Details

- Ask students to work individually and then compare answers in pairs.
- Check answers as a class.

Answer Key

1. zooplankton, anchoveta, shrimp, and clams
2. they produce oxygen
3. 100 pounds
4. He is trying to save the things that we rely on the ocean for.

Exercise D. | Critical Thinking: Analyzing Problems and Solutions

- Draw students' attention to the **CT Focus** box. Explain that asking these questions after reading will help students to critically evaluate the arguments in a text.
- Ask volunteers to write their ideas on the board.

Answer Key

1. eat farm-raised fish, eat fish that are low on the food chain; stop eating bigger fish

2. help to raise awareness of problems facing the world's oceans; think more carefully about what we eat

Exercise E. | Critical Thinking: Synthesizing

Have students discuss the questions in groups. Then lead a brief class discussion and have students share their ideas.

Exploring Written English

45 mins *(pages 75–76)*

Exercise A. | Brainstorming

- Have students work in pairs to write words or phrases.
- Walk around the class as students work and help them with ideas as needed. (Possible answers: weather maps, economic forecasts, gas and electricity usage)

Exercise B. | Journal Writing

- Allow time for students to write their answers individually.
- Walk around as students write, offering help or suggestions as needed.

> **TIP** Bring in examples of charts and graphs from everyday life (from newspapers, magazines, bills, etc.) to illustrate this lesson.

Exercise C. | Analyzing

- Go over the information in the box. Point out that this skill is often required for academic writing and is frequently tested on academic English exams.
- Have students complete the sentences.
- Ask volunteers to read out their answers.

Answer Key

1. quadrupled
2. increased/rose
3. decreased/declined/dipped/dropped/fell
4. remained stable/steady/stayed the same

Exercise D. | Applying

Monitor students as they work, and help them with ideas as needed.

Writing Skill: Explaining a Chart or Graph

Go over the information in the box. Point out the difference between a chart and a graph, referring to examples in this unit.

Exercise E. | Critical Thinking: Analyzing

- Ask some questions about the chart. For example, *What does the y axis show?* (sea level changes in cm) *What does the x axis show?* (sea level rise between the years 1880 and 2000)

- Discuss the incorrect sentences and write the correct answers on the board.
- Draw students' attention to the **Strategy** box. Identify the most recent piece of data in this and in previous graphs in the unit.
- Monitor students as they work in pairs, and provide assistance as needed.
- Check answers as a class and reach agreement on the best criteria for ordering the sentences. (The main idea is first, and then they appear chronologically.)

Answer Key

Sentences 3 and 4 are not correct. Corrections are shown in bold.
3. After 1910, it began to **rise** steadily.
4. By the year 2000, sea level reached almost **20** centimeters.

Answer Key

1, 5, 3, 2, 4
According to the graph, sea level rose about 20 centimeters over 120 years. Between 1880 and 1910, it went up and down slightly, but it remained fairly stable. After 1910, it began to rise steadily. Sea level rose about 10 centimeters in the 50 years between 1910 and 1960. By the year 2000, sea level reached almost 20 centimeters.

Writing Task: Drafting *(page 77)*

Exercise A. | Planning

- Go over the steps in this exercise.
- Remind students that complete sentences are not necessary at this stage and that it is more important to focus on their ideas than on grammar or spelling.
- Walk around and monitor students' work. Provide assistance as needed.

Exercise B. | Draft 1

- Ask students to look back at pages 75–76 to find useful language for this task. Write some useful phrases on the board for reference.
- Walk around and monitor students as they work. Provide assistance as needed.

> **TIP** If higher-level students finish early, ask them to write a paragraph describing another graph or chart in this unit.

Writing Task: Revising *(page 78)*

Exercise C. | Analyzing

- Allow time for students to read both paragraphs and compare them.
- Ask volunteers to describe the differences between the two paragraphs.

Answer Key

Paragraph a is the first draft. Paragraph b is the revision. Students may find the following differences:
Paragraph a says that salmon farming began in the 1950s and grew quickly in the next 50 years. In fact, it did not start to grow until 1980.

Paragraph a contains inaccurate numerical amounts. Paragraph a ends with a personal opinion, which is irrelevant to the main idea and not appropriate to the description of a graph.

Exercise D. | Critical Thinking: Analysis

- Ask students to work in pairs to discuss their answers.
- Go over the answers together as a class.

Answer Key

	a	b
1.	N	Y
2.	Y	Y
3.	Y	Y
4.	Y	N
5.	N	Y
6.	N	Y

Exercise E. | Revising

- Remind students that asking the questions in exercise **D** will help them to improve their own writing.
- Walk around and monitor students as they work. Provide assistance as needed.

> **TIP** After monitoring students' work, you may want to list on the board some of the unit vocabulary or other extra vocabulary that you feel will be helpful to students when they write their second draft.

Exercise F. | Peer Evaluation

- Go over the four steps in the evaluation process to make sure students know what to do.
- Remind students that positive feedback is just as important as constructive criticism.

Exercise G. | Draft 2

Monitor students as they work, and provide assistance as needed.

Exercise H. | Editing Practice

- Go over the information in the box, and then have students edit the four sentences.
- Allow time for students to read the sentences.
- Check the answers by asking students to read out the correct sentences and explain the errors.

Answer Key

1. Between 1991 and 1992, production of Atlantic salmon **declined** slightly.
2. Production of Atlantic salmon doubled **between** 1990 and 1995.
3. (correct)
4. Production of Atlantic salmon increased by about 1.4 million tonnes **in** 30 years.

Writing Task: Editing *(page 80)*

Exercise I. | Editing Checklist

- Go over the sentences in the editing checklist.
- Allow time for students to read and edit their work.

Exercise J. | Final Draft

Allow time for students to work on their final draft, and then collect their work.

Unit Quiz

- Students can work in groups to answer the questions.
- Encourage students to refer back to the relevant pages
  of the unit to find the answers.
- To do the quiz as a competition, have students work in teams.

Answer Key

1. human activities	**5.** people
2. ecosystem	**6.** oxygen
3. overfishing	**7.** steady, stable
4. x and y axes	**8.** main idea, purpose

IDEAS FOR... **Vocabulary Review**

Use a puzzle website to make a crossword with vocabulary from this unit.

Make two versions of the crossword. Student A's crossword should include some words and clues that are missing on Student B's puzzle. Student B's puzzle should include words and clues that are missing on Student A's puzzle. Have students work in pairs to complete the two puzzles.

IDEAS FOR... **Journal Writing**

At the end of this unit, ask students to write about: a) the criteria they use for choosing the food they eat; b) a diet with and without meat or fish; or c) some of their own ideas for solving the problems facing the world's oceans.

IDEAS FOR... **Further Research**

Ask students to find out about other organizations that are trying to help protect and conserve the world's oceans.

Memory and Learning

Academic Track
Health Science/
Psychology

Academic Pathways:
Lesson A: Identifying cause and effect in an
expository text
Lesson B: Synthesizing information from multiple texts
Lesson C: Using an outline to plan a paragraph
Writing a paragraph with supporting
information

Unit Theme

Why do we remember some things and not others? Why do some people have better memories than others?

Unit 5 explores the theme of memory as it relates to:

– memory in ancient times and now
– techniques for memorization

– tips to improve memory
– the connection between memory and sleep

Think and Discuss *(page 81)*

- Ask students to describe the pictures. Ask if they enjoy taking photographs. When do they take pictures and why? (Possible answers: on special occasions, trips, birthdays, etc.) What do they do with the pictures? (Possible answers: store them on CDs or on their computer, make albums or scrapbooks, send them to friends and family) Do they see taking pictures as an art form, or simply as a way of remembering the past?

- Have students discuss the questions in groups.

- Ask volunteers to tell the class about the interesting ideas and experiences their classmates described.

Exploring the Theme
(pages 82–83)

The opening spread features a selection of objects left by visitors to a war memorial in Maryland, USA.

- Point out the caption on page 82 and ask students why they think people left these objects. (Possible ideas: A war memorial is a place to remember soldiers who have died in a war. People sometimes leave personal objects at a memorial as a way of remembering a family member or friend who died in war. The objects may be things the soldier owned or liked.)

- Ask students to name the objects in the picture and suggest what personal significance they may have had to the people who left them there. (Possible

answers: medals, a toy car, a high-heeled shoe, a lighter, photographs, books, dog tags [military identification tags], a fan, letters, a baseball)

- Read questions A1–2. Have students close their books and write as many items as they can remember. Which items did everyone remember? Were there any that everyone forgot?

- Go over the information in the box and discuss questions B1–2 as a class.

Answer Key

B1. Possible answers:
Short-term: telephone numbers, names of people we have just met
Long-term: childhood memories, things that happened long ago
B2. Our ability to recall peaks at the age of 32 and then starts to decline gradually as we get older.

IDEAS FOR... Expansion

Ask students to write a one-sentence description of their earliest memory on a piece of paper (without signing their name). Collect all the papers and lay them out randomly on a table. Ask students to read them. Try to classify them—for example, memories connected with food, family, school, or holidays. Discuss what makes an experience memorable.

30 mins

Preparing to Read *(page 84)*

WARM-UP

The Lesson A target vocabulary is presented through a matching exercise.

Ask students to think about things they use in their daily lives that help them remember. Brainstorm possible answers and write them on the board. (Possible answers: calendars, clocks, photographs, lists, etc.)

Exercise A. | Building Vocabulary

- Remind students of ways to use context clues to guess meaning: a) look at the meaning of any prefixes or suffixes; b) guess what part of speech the word is; and c) look at key words in the sentence or previous sentence for clues to the definition.

- Draw attention to the **Word Link** box. Ask students to suggest definitions for each of the additional words. Have students use their dictionaries for any words they can't figure out.

- Ask students to think of some other examples of verbs ending in –*ize*. (Possible answers: *internationalize, organize, recognize, socialize*)

- Ask students to find other forms for some of the words in exercise **A**. (Possible answers: *(n.)* complexity; *(n.)* visualization; *(n.)* memorization; *(v.)* achieve)

- Check the answers by asking volunteers to read out a definition each.

Answer Key

1. technique	**6.** internal
2. genius	**7.** external
3. collective knowledge	**8.** complex
4. visualize	**9.** achievement
5. memorize	**10.** texts

Exercise B. | Using Vocabulary

Invite volunteers to share their answers with the class.

Answer Key

Possible answers:
1. history, mythology, traditions
2. Leonardo da Vinci, Albert Einstein, Stephen Hawking, Pablo Picasso
3. noise, heat or cold, bad lighting

Exercise C. | Classifying

- Ask students to name some examples of things that you can make lists for and things that you memorize.

- Have students work in pairs and then share their ideas with the class.

Answer Key

Possible answers:
Things I make lists for: things I need to buy at the supermarket or the drugstore, directions to a new place, new vocabulary words, housework, and other things I have to do in a day/week

Things I try to memorize: friends' and relatives' birthdays, phone numbers and addresses that I use often, passwords

> **TIP** If students have trouble with exercise C, write a list of possible items on the board and have students classify them—for example, dates, names, things to do, vocabulary words, shopping, friends' and relatives' birthdays, phone numbers, things to take on vacation.

Exercise D. | Predicting

- Point out the **Strategy** box. Remind students that scanning is reading through a text quickly to find specific information.

- Note: Students will check their predictions later, in exercise **A** on page 87.

Answer Key

Possible answers:
memory, remember, memorize

track **1-12**

Ask students to read the passage. Point out that the vocabulary definitions in the footnotes on pages 85 and 86 will help them understand the reading.

Overview of the Reading

The reading passage describes how attitudes toward memory have changed over the centuries; it also explains a special technique for memorization called the loci method.

Understanding the Reading
(page 87)

Exercise A. | Understanding the Gist

Check students' predictions in exercise **D** on page 84. Did they guess the general idea correctly?

> **Answer Key**
>
> Possible answer:
> how attitudes toward memory have changed over the centuries

Exercise B. | Identifying Key Details

- Allow time for students to go back to the reading and write the answers individually and then compare them in pairs.
- Check the answers by inviting volunteers to read out their answers.

> **Answer Key**
>
> Possible answers:
> 1. Because it is a skill that few people have. / Because they respected people who could remember large amounts of data.
> 2. You can remember a sequence of tasks by associating them with a very familiar place.

Exercise C. | Critical Thinking: Applying a Method

- Point out the **CT Focus** box. Explain that trying to solve the two problems in exercise **C** using the loci method will help them understand better how it works.
- Ask students to work in small groups and think of how they might use the loci method to solve one or both of the problems. Then have groups share their ideas.

Exercise D. | Classifying

Ask for one or two examples.

> **Answer Key**
>
> Internal Memory: loci method, visualization
> External Memory: photographs, calendars, schedules, books, Internet, notepads, iPads

Exercise E. | Critical Thinking: Inferring Opinion

- Remind students that making inferences involves thinking about meanings that are not directly stated.
- Ask students if they think the author would answer this question affirmatively or negatively and why they think so. (Possible answer: The author might agree that we have lost an important skill. The author describes the art of memory in ancient times with respect and admiration, but seems less enthusiastic about the use of technological crutches.)

Exercise F. | Personalizing

- Ask students to work individually and then compare answers in pairs.
- Discuss the questions as a class, comparing answers and opinions.
- Ask students to write an entry in their journal summarizing the role of memory in ancient times and today.

> **IDEAS FOR...** Checking Comprehension
>
> Ask students to summarize the main idea of each paragraph.

> **IDEAS FOR...** Expansion
>
> Have students exchange tips and ideas for remembering words, facts, and other data useful for their studies. Make a class list of the top 10 tips.

Developing Reading Skills

45 mins

(page 88)

Reading Skill: Identifying Cause and Effect

- Go over the information in the box.
- If you think it is helpful, draw a diagram on the board with arrows to show the relationship between cause and effect.
- If necessary, extend the presentation by giving some examples from the previous unit—for example, *Is overfishing the cause or the effect of disappearing fish species? What are some of the effects of disappearing fish species?*

Exercise A. | Analyzing

track **1-13**

- Ask if students know the colors of the rainbow. If not, see if they can associate the name of a color with each of the letters in the illustration.
- Allow time for students to read the passage. Have them work individually to circle and underline their answers.
- After checking the answers, point out the **CT Focus** box. Brainstorm words with *ie* or *ei* and write them on the board. (Examples that follow the rule: *believe, achieve, ceiling, deceive.* Exceptions to the rule: *seize, leisure*)
- Ask if students know of any other memory tricks (for example, acronyms or rhymes) in English or in their own language.
- Check the answers as a class.

Pronunciation Note

The initial *m* in the word *mnemonic* is silent.

Answer Key

1. Cause: people often use things like poems, pictures, or movements
   Effect: it is easier to remember rhymes, images, and actions
2. Cause: acronyms are short
   Effect: they are easier to remember
3. Cause: English spelling rules can be difficult to learn
   Effect: some students use rhymes to help them remember the rules
4. Cause: by learning "*i* before *e* except after *c* (where you hear *ee*)"
   Effect: students of English remember the spelling of words like *niece* and *receipt*

Exercise B. | Analyzing

Allow time for students to read and write their ideas individually and then compare answers in pairs. Encourage them to ask each other questions to help them identify the causes and effects. For example: *What caused Simonides to develop the loci method?*

Answer Key

1. Cause: Simonides realized that it's easier to remember places and locations
   Effect: he developed the loci method
2. Cause: Peter of Ravenna used the loci method to remember books and poems
   Effect: he was able to reread books stored in the "memory palaces" of his mind
3. Cause: books and pens were not available
   Effect: people had to memorize what they learned
4. Cause: We have photographs, calendars, books, and the Internet
   Effect: we don't have to remember anything anymore

Viewing: Memory School
(page 89)

Overview of the Video

This video is about the type of training that London taxi drivers have to do before they can qualify as drivers. They have to memorize routes and locations of buildings so that they can find their way around London quickly and easily.

Before Viewing

Exercise A. | Meaning from Context

- Have students work in pairs to discuss and write definitions of the words and phrases.
- Compare answers as a class.

Answer Key

1. change, continue to have
2. dealing with things that you see
3. find their way, a map in their mind, memorable places

Exercise B. | Brainstorming

Ask volunteers to write their ideas on the board. (Possible answers: use a GPS, refer to a map, consult a guidebook)

While Viewing

Exercises A and B.

- Ask students to read the questions in exercises **A** and **B**.
- Play the video. Ask students to check their answers in the Brainstorming exercise in Before Viewing, and to write short answers to questions 1–4 in exercise **B**.

Answer Key

1. They use a complex mental map.
2. They ride a bike around London and memorize the roads and the landmarks.
3. It could help stroke victims, or people with Alzheimer's or brain damage.
4. Remembering faces, pictures, and diagrams might enlarge the hippocampus.

Vocabulary Notes

mate = colloquial term for *friend*
instantly = immediately
significantly = greatly
hippocampus = part of the brain responsible for storing and retrieving memories
bit by bit = gradually
stroke = when a blood clot prevents blood flow to the brain, sometimes causing severe brain damage
Alzheimer's = a condition in which a person's brain gradually stops working properly

After Viewing

Exercise A.

- Have students discuss and compare answers.
- Play the video again and check answers as a class.

Exercise B. | Critical Thinking: Synthesizing

Have students work in pairs, referring back to the reading as necessary, and then discuss the answers as a class.

Answer Key

Possible answers:
These two techniques are different because the loci method uses locations to remember other types of information, while the London taxi drivers are remembering actual locations. The techniques are similar in that they both use visual memory.

Preparing to Read *(pages 90–91)*

 track **1-14**

30 mins

WARM-UP

The Lesson B target vocabulary is presented in a matching exercise.

Ask students if they have any tips for improving memory. (Possible answers: eat a healthy diet, stay active, etc.)

Exercise A. | Building Vocabulary

- Do the first item together with the class as an example.
- Point out the **Word Partners** box. Remind students that these word partners are sometimes called collocations.
- After checking answers with the class, point out the **Word Link** box. Ask students for further examples. (Possible answers: *transmit, transport, transcribe, transfusion*)

Answer Key

1. a **2.** a **3.** a **4.** a **5.** a **6.** b **7.** b **8.** a **9.** a **10.** a

---

IDEAS FOR... Multi-level Classes

To make exercise **A** more challenging, suggest that students cover the choices and try to define the target vocabulary without looking at them. Then they can uncover the choices to check their answers.

Exercise B. | Using Vocabulary

- Give an example of your own for the first item.
- Allow time for students to complete the answers individually and then compare answers in pairs.
- Ask one student from each pair to summarize their answers.
- Take notes of any common errors, and provide feedback.
- Ask if students agree with the top five causes of stress. If not, what other causes would they suggest?

TIP For question 1 of exercise B, lead a brief class discussion on ways to cope with stress in students' lives.

Exercise C. | Predicting

- Point out the **Strategy** box. Ask students to identify the key words from the titles and subheads in the reading.
- Note: Students will check their predictions later, in exercise **A** on page 94.

Ask students to read the article. Remind them that the vocabulary definitions in the footnotes at the bottom of page 92 are there to help them understand the reading.

Overview of the Reading

The reading consists of two short articles on the theme of memory. The first article gives four tips for improving your memory:

- reduce stress
- play brain games
- get enough sleep
- eat the right food

The second article explains how the brain transfers memories to the hippocampus while we sleep.

Further information about sleep and memory can be found here:
http://newswatch.nationalgeographic.com/2009/08/26/why_we_sleep_is_a_mystery/

and here:

http://newswatch.nationalgeographic.com/2011/10/08/inside-the-secrets-of-illusions-memory/

IDEAS FOR... Checking Comprehension

Ask these additional questions or write them on the board:

1. What are some other ways of reducing or avoiding stress?

2. What are some other examples of brainteasers?

3. What are some other examples of motor skills?

4. What are some other examples of foods rich in antioxidants?

5. Describe the experiments with rats in your own words.

6. Describe the graph in your own words.

After completing the exercises on page 94, you may want to discuss these questions or assign them as journal-writing tasks for homework.

1. What advice would you give to yourself about improving your memory?

2. Have you ever gone without sleep for a long period of time? What effects did you notice?

3. What are some of your strongest memories, and why do you remember them?

Understanding the Reading
(page 94)

Exercise A. | Understanding the Gist

Check students' predictions in exercise **C** on page 91.

Answer Key

1. . . . we can improve our memory through mental and physical exercise and good lifestyle choices.

2. . . . the brain activity that happens during sleep creates long-term memories.

Exercise B. | Identifying Key Ideas

Ask students to tell you which part of the passage gives the answers.

Answer Key

antioxidants (paragraph E), puzzles (paragraph C), sleep (paragraph D)

Exercise C. | Understanding the Main Idea

- Ask students to work in pairs to complete the sentence.
- Check answers as a class.

Answer Key

Possible answer:
. . . sleep is important for learning and memory; the Rutgers study also explains how the brain makes long-term memories.

Exercise D. | Restating Key Details

- Point out the **Strategy** box. Ask students to underline the key words and phrases in the three questions.
- Remind students that scanning involves reading quickly while looking for specific information.

Answer Key

1. . . . a type of brain activity that happens during sleep.
2. . . . hippocampus, neocortex
3. . . . a drug stopped them from storing memories during sleep.

Exercise E. | Matching Cause and Effect

- Discuss the answer as a class.
- Ask students to work in pairs to find two other cause-effect relationships in the reading.
- Walk around and monitor students' discussions. Provide assistance as needed.

Answer Key

1. a (stress causes people to forget things)
2. Possible answers:
Cause = the drug
Effect = stopped the rats' brainwave activity
Cause = lack of sleep
Effect = the rats had trouble remembering the route

Exercise F. | Critical Thinking: Synthesizing

- Have students discuss the questions in small groups.
- Point out that this exercise will help students with the writing task in the next lesson.

Answer Key

1. visualization, acronyms, rhymes and other mnemonics, using a mental map, avoiding stress, brain puzzles, getting enough sleep, eating the right food

2. They know how the brain transfers memories during sleep and the role the hippocampus plays in making long-term memories.

45 mins

Exploring Written English *(pages 95–96)*

Exercise A. | Brainstorming

- Review the four steps in the writing process: planning, writing, revising, and editing.

- After students have brainstormed ideas in pairs, ask volunteers to write their ideas on the board. (Possible answers: brain-training exercises, word associations, making up a story that includes new words you want to remember)

Exercise B. | Journal Writing

- Point out that this exercise will help students with their writing task in the next part of the lesson.

- Allow time for students to work individually. Walk around as students write, and offer help or suggestions as needed. If necessary, ask questions to help students expand their ideas.

TIP Divide the class into groups and give each group a sheet of poster paper where they can write their tips for improving memory. They can add drawings and other designs to illustrate their posters. If possible, display the posters in the classroom.

Exercise C. | Language for Writing

- Go over the information in the box.

- Remind students how to form the gerund, referring them to the spelling rules on page 217. Then have students make two more sentences with the stem *You can improve your memory* (by doing brain puzzles, by visualizing places, etc.).

- Allow time for students to complete their answers individually.

- Check the answers as a class. Then ask volunteers to write the sentences on the board, this time reversing the order of the *by* + gerund forms.

Answer Key

1. By writing new words on cards, a person can retain them better.
2. By giving rats drugs, the scientists stopped their brain waves.
3. You can improve your memory by doing puzzles.

Exercise D.

Allow time for students to write their sentences individually. This can be assigned as homework.

IDEAS FOR... Practicing Grammar

Collect students' work from exercise **D** and select ten sentences. Write each sentence in two parts on two strips of paper. Spread them out on a large table. Then invite students to gather around the table and match up the two parts of the sentences.

Writing Skill: Using an Outline *(page 96)*

- Go over the information in the box.

- Find out which students already use an outline when they gather and organize ideas before writing.

- Discuss the advantages of using an outline.

Exercise E. | Matching

- Allow time for students to work individually to match the sentences to the parts of the outline. Tell them to circle the letters of the two extra sentences.

- Walk around and monitor students as they work. Provide assistance as needed.

- Check answers as a class.

Answer Key

Topic sentence: a
Supporting idea 1: b
Details: c, d
Supporting idea 2: e
Details: g, h
Sentences f and i are extra.

Exercise F. | Critical Thinking: Analyzing

After checking answers with the class, give additional practice by asking volunteers to cover the paragraph and paraphrase the information using the outline.

Answer Key

Sentence f uses paraphrasing and sentence i provides a concluding statement.

Exercise G.

Have volunteers read the cause-effect relationships they underlined. Does the class agree?

Answer Key

Possible answers:
Cause: creating a mental picture of it
Effect: memorize a route
Cause: seeing the route in your mind
Effect: you will learn it faster

Writing Task: Drafting *(page 97)*

Exercise A. | Planning

- Go over the steps in this exercise.
- Point out the numbering and lettering system used to organize the outline. Numbers are for points that support the topic sentence/main idea. Letters are for examples and/or details of the supporting ideas.
- Walk around and monitor students' work. Provide assistance as needed.
- Select some good topic sentences and supporting ideas and read them aloud without mentioning whose they are.

Exercise B. | Draft 1

Allow time for students to work individually.

> **TIP** Remind students to focus on content and organization of ideas at this stage. Questions about grammar and vocabulary will be dealt with at the next stage.

Writing Task: Revising *(page 98)*

Exercise C. | Analyzing

- You may wish to introduce this exercise by going over the questions in exercise **D**.
- Ask students to work in pairs to discuss the questions.
- Have volunteers explain the reasons for their choices.

Answer Key

Paragraph a is the first draft. Paragraph b is the revision.

Paragraph b has a strong topic sentence that gives a clear overview of the paragraph. It also has a good concluding sentence that sums up the paragraph.

Paragraph a has neither a topic sentence nor a concluding sentence.

Exercise D. | Critical Thinking: Analysis

- Do the first item together as an example. What is the main idea of the paragraph? (how people can record important events in life so the events will become lasting memories)
- Ask students to discuss the questions in pairs.
- Go over the answers together as a class.
- Point out the **CT Focus** box. Ask students to look back at page 86. Have volunteers identify the topic sentences, the supporting ideas, and the examples and/or details.
- If time allows, ask students to prepare an outline of this paragraph.

Answer Key

	a	b
1.	Y	Y
2.	N	Y
3.	Y	Y
4.	N	Y
5.	Y	N
6.	N	Y

Exercise E. | Revising

- Remind students that asking the questions in exercise **D** will help them improve their own writing.
- Walk around and monitor students as they work. Provide assistance as needed.

Writing Task: Editing *(page 99)*

Exercise F. | Peer Evaluation

- Quickly discuss the four steps in this exercise.
- The purpose of this exercise is to see if the writer has managed to convey the ideas set out in his or her outline.

> **TIP** If students have difficulty giving positive feedback, suggest some useful phrases. For example: *I thought . . . was really interesting. I liked the way you explained . . . . I think you included some excellent examples.*

Exercise G. | Draft 2

Monitor students as they work, and provide assistance as needed.

> **TIP** While monitoring students' work, you may want to list on the board some of the unit vocabulary or other extra vocabulary that you feel might be valuable for students' writing.

Exercise H. | Editing Practice

- Go over the information in the box and then have students edit the four sentences.
- Check the answers by asking students to read out the correct sentences and explain the errors.

Answer Key

1. You can't remember all of the information by just **listening** to a lecture.
2. By **taking** notes while you listen, you can remember information better.
3. By doing a motor activity while you listen**,** you can improve your memory.
4. By **writing** a summary of your notes after a lecture, you will remember the information more easily.

Writing Task: Editing
(pages 99–100)

Exercise I. | Editing Checklist

- Read the sentences in the editing checklist.
- Have volunteers give examples of each type of error.
- Allow time for students to read and edit their work.

Exercise J. | Final Draft

Have students complete their third draft and then collect their work.

Unit Quiz

- Students can work in groups to answer the questions.
- Encourage students to refer back to the relevant pages of the unit to find the answers.
- To do the quiz as a competition, you can have students work in teams.

Answer Key

1. cells	5. external
2. short-term	6. effect
3. technique	7. acronym
4. loci method	8. long-term

IDEAS FOR... Evaluation

It may be helpful for students if you show them the grading rubric that you will use to evaluate their work.

Alternatively, you may want to work together with your students to collaboratively develop a grading rubric.

You could also compare different rubrics from examinations that your students may take in the future.

IDEAS FOR... Journal Writing

Ask students to write about a) the advice they would give someone for remembering vocabulary, facts, and other data useful for their studies; b) a comparison between two different types of memory—for example, remembering dates and remembering how to play the piano; or c) one of their earliest memories and the reason they think they still remember the experience.

IDEAS FOR... Further Research

Ask students to find out about other research on memory and the brain and to write a short report about what they find out. They can present their reports in the next class.

Dangerous Cures

Academic Track
Medicine

Academic Pathways:

Lesson A: Identifying pros and cons
Identifying figurative language
Lesson B: Reading a biographical account
Lesson C: Showing both sides of an issue
Writing a persuasive paragraph

Unit Theme

Most people are afraid of being stung or bitten by animals, especially poisonous ones. While poisons, or toxins, from some animals are dangerous and sometimes deadly, some toxins have a positive function—they are used as medicine to cure people.

Unit 6 explores the topic of medical research as it relates to:

– collecting toxins from snakes and frogs
– toxins: their benefits and dangers
– rebuilding and researching extinct viruses
– animal testing

Think and Discuss *(page 101)*

- Ask students to describe the picture. What adjectives would they use to describe the tarantula? Refer students to the caption. What do they think is happening? (A scientist is taking out the spider's venom, or poison.) Ask what students already know about tarantulas. Have people in the class ever seen a tarantula? If so, have them describe the situation.

- Discuss question 1 as a class. You might share your own experience with the class first—for example, If you were ever stung or bitten, how did it happen? What kind of animal was it? What did you do?

- Discuss question 2. Make a word web on the board and write students' suggestions. (Possible answers: medicine, vaccinations, weapons, scientific research)

Note: A tarantula is a large hairy spider found in most continents of the world including North and South America, Africa, Asia, and Australia. All tarantulas are poisonous, but most are harmless to humans. Only some species have venom that can produce extreme discomfort over a period of several days. Some species are popular as exotic pets.

Exploring the Theme

(pages 102–103)

The opening spread features information about poisonous animals.

- Ask students to look at the pictures and read the information about each animal. Then ask a few questions to check comprehension—for example, Which animal is just two inches long? Which animal lives in Australia? Which animal lives in the ocean?

- Discuss questions 1–3. For question 1, you may want to discuss which animal is the most attractive or the ugliest. Which animal is the scariest?

Answer Key

1. Answers will vary.

2. The poison dart frog, the taipan, and the black widow are deadly to humans.

3. They all produce a type of toxin used for self-defense. The animals all produce a different type of toxin, but not all of the toxins are deadly to humans. Some of the animals use venom to attack other animals by stinging or biting, and others use toxins to protect themselves from predators.

> **TIP** After reading the information, have students work in pairs. One partner closes his or her book while the other asks questions about the animals. Alternatively, ask students to close their books. Read out one or two facts about each animal, asking students to remember which animal it is.

IDEAS FOR... Expansion

Ask students to write in their journals about an experience with a dangerous, scary, or unusual animal.

---

30 mins

Preparing to Read *(page 104)*

WARM-UP

The Lesson A target vocabulary is presented in a box. Students will use the vocabulary to complete sentences after trying to guess their meaning from context in the reading *The Snake Chaser*.

Ask students to look at the photograph on page 105 and describe it. What do they think the man's job is?

Exercise A. | Building Vocabulary

- Ask students to read the words in the box and check (✓) the words they know and underline the ones they aren't sure about.

- Have students find the words they don't know in the reading and use the other words around them to guess their meanings. Then have them complete the sentences using the words in the box.

- Check the answers by asking volunteers to read a sentence each.

- Point out the **Word Link** box. Discuss the meanings of these words and ask for further examples with the prefix *dis-*. (Possible answers: *disapprove, displeasure, disbelieve, dislike*)

TIP Have students tell you the part of speech for each item. This will help them understand the meaning of the word in the sentence.

Answer Key

1. specific	**6.** encounter
2. target	**7.** cure
3. disease	**8.** model
4. colleague	**9.** resources
5. endangered	**10.** side effects

IDEAS FOR... Expansion

Have students use the target vocabulary to write their own example sentences in their vocabulary notebooks.

Exercise B. | Using Vocabulary

Invite volunteers to share their answers with the class. (Possible answers: 1. whale, polar bear, panda; 2. cancer, AIDS, Parkinson's, Alzheimer's; 3. library, computer, Internet, newspaper)

Exercise C. | Brainstorming

After students complete their answers individually, have them compare answers in pairs. (Possible answers: scientific research, experiments on animals and humans)

Exercise D. | Predicting

- Draw attention to the **Strategy** box. Ask volunteers to read out the title, the captions, and the opening sentences.

- Note: Students will check their prediction later, in exercise **A** on page 107.

track 2-01 Ask students to read the passage. Remind them that the vocabulary definitions in the footnotes at the bottom of pages 105 and 106 will help them understand the reading.

Overview of the Reading

The passage describes the work of Zoltan Takacs and his colleagues, who collect venom for scientific research from snakes around the world. Takacs believes that toxins can help cure many diseases. He is afraid that if species disappear, the opportunity to develop these cures will disappear, too.

Understanding the Reading
(page 107)

Exercise A. | Understanding the Gist

- Check students' prediction in exercise **D** on page 104. Did they guess the general idea correctly? (a person's job)
- Have students answer the question individually and then compare answers in pairs.
- Check the answer as a class.

Answer Key

The correct answer is item b. Although the other two sentences are true, they do not give the gist, or general point, of the article.

Vocabulary Notes

tell the difference (paragraph C) = differentiate, distinguish
potentially (paragraph E) = possibly
biodiversity (paragraph F) = the existence of a wide variety of animal and plant species living in their natural environment

Exercise B. | Identifying Key Details

- Explain that students should write the second part of each sentence, giving a reason for the first part.
- Do the first item together as an example.
- Allow time for students to work individually and then compare answers in pairs.
- Check answers as a class.

Answer Key

1. . . . he wants to find out if their venom can be used to cure people.

2. . . . they can hit a single target.

3. . . . they help researchers identify which toxin might cure a specific disease more quickly.

4. . . . researchers can test many toxins at once.

5. . . . every time an animal becomes extinct, a new drug may be lost, too.

6. . . . they have a molecule that blocks the venom from making contact.

Exercise C. | Critical Thinking: Identifying Figurative Language

- Point out the **CT Focus** box. Give some examples of figurative language—for example, *You are what you eat.* The literal meaning is that you are food, but the figurative meaning is that you need to eat good food to be healthy.
- Explain that the words *like* and *as* often indicate figurative language because they compare two things—for example, *His <u>voice</u> was loud like <u>thunder</u>.*

> **TIP** You may want to explain the difference between a simile and a metaphor, the two most common types of figurative language. A simile compares two things (usually using *as* or *like*)—for example, *She's as busy as a bee.* A metaphor substitutes one thing for another—for example, *She's a busy bee.*

Answer Key   1. b 2. b 3. b

Exercise D. | Personalizing

When students finish writing their answers, discuss the questions as a class.

IDEAS FOR...   Checking Comprehension

Ask these questions or write them on the board.
1. Why is Zoltan's job difficult? (His trips are often dangerous.)
2. Why do many drugs produce side effects? (Because the drugs affect more than one target.)
3. How do scientists use the toxin libraries? (To identify which toxin might cure a specific disease.)
4. Why are Zoltan and his team worried about the future? (Because we will lose potential drugs as animals become extinct.)

Developing Reading Skills

45 mins

(page 108)

Reading Skill: Identifying Pros and Cons

- Go over the information in the box.
- Ask students to write the main points in their notebooks. For example:

Pros — positive points

Cons — negative points

Pros and cons . . .

– present a more balanced argument

– help to evaluate an argument

– help you decide your own opinion

track **2-02**

Exercise A. | Identifying Pros and Cons

- Have students read the title of the passage. Have them read the first footnote that explains what a virus is. Explain that a dead virus is one that no longer causes disease. Ask students why scientists might want to make a dead virus alive again. Do they think this is a good or bad idea?
- Ask students to read the text and complete the chart.

Answer Key

Pros: We can learn about how viruses cause disease. We can learn about how humans developed in the past. We can develop vaccines in case they reappear. Cons: It is very dangerous because viruses could infect the scientists and researchers. Viruses could escape and infect large numbers of people.

Exercise B. | Evaluating Arguments

When students have finished writing, discuss the answers as a class. You might want to discuss what kinds of restrictions would have to be placed on scientists doing this kind of research in order to do it safely.

> **IDEAS FOR...** **Expansion**
>
> Ask this question or write it on the board:
> What are the pros and cons of testing drugs on animals?
> (Possible answers: Pro: We can test drugs and save human lives. Con: Animals can suffer.)

Viewing: The Frog Licker
(page 109)

Overview of the Video

The video describes the work of scientist Valerie Clark, who studies frogs to find out about toxins that could be valuable for medical research. The Mantella poison frog in Madagascar is particularly interesting because it has a variety of toxins that are produced from the insects the frog eats.

Vocabulary Notes

Madagascar = an island country in the Indian Ocean off the southeastern coast of Africa
lemur = animal that is like a monkey, with large eyes and a long tail
amphibian = animal that lives in water when young and on land as an adult
millipede = a long insect, similar to a centipede, with a lot of legs
mite = a very tiny insect, almost invisible to the human eye, that sometimes lives on other insects
GPS = Global Positioning System, a satellite navigations system that provides precise location information
the season for love = the mating season

Before Viewing

Exercise A. | Meaning from Context

- Ask students to look at the picture and suggest reasons why the person is licking a frog.
- Ask students what they know about Madagascar. Where is it? (See world globe next to title.) What is special about it? What animals live there?
- Have students work individually to match the definitions of the words. Then ask students to compare answers and discuss the meaning of the sentence.
- Compare answers as a class.

Answer Key

1. C 2. B 3. A
The sentence describes two things happening at the same time, where one encourages the other. This can be rephrased as: If there is more primary forest, there will be a better chance of finding new drugs.

Exercise B. | Predicting

Ask volunteers to write their ideas on the board. (Possible answers: how they make toxins, what they eat, how they reproduce, what helps them survive)

While Viewing

Exercises A and B.

- Ask students to read the questions in exercises **A** and **B**.
- Play the video. Ask students to check their answers to the Brainstorming exercise in Before Viewing and to write short answers to questions 1–4 in exercise **B**.

Answer Key

1. The toxins are a side effect of the frog's diet.
2. She wipes its back with tissue soaked in alcohol. / She gives it a quick lick to see if it tastes bitter.
3. It is only mildly poisonous to humans.
4. There will be a smaller number of toxins available to study for medical research.

After Viewing

Exercise A.

- Have students discuss and compare answers.
- Play the video again and check the answers.

Exercise B. | Critical Thinking: Synthesizing

Ask students to work in pairs, referring back to the reading as necessary, and then discuss the answers as a class.

Answer Key

Possible answers:
They both have difficult jobs and have to travel to faraway places. They both have the goal of helping medical research. Zoltan's job is more dangerous because some snakes are deadlier to humans than most frogs.

Preparing to Read

30 mins

(pages 110–111)

WARM-UP

The Lesson B target vocabulary is introduced through sentences that present the words in context. Students are asked to identify each word's part of speech and then write its meaning.

Exercise A. | Building Vocabulary

- Do the first item together with the class as an example. (The sentence gives two examples of careers: biologist and virologist.)
- Allow time for students to work individually or in pairs.
- Point out the **Word Partners** box. Ask students for example situations when they might use each of the expressions.

Answer Key

1. noun; a job or profession that someone does for a long period of his or her life
2. noun; actions that produce something or make something successful
3. noun; limit
4. verb; shows the difference between two things
5. noun; a measured amount of a medicine or drug to be taken at one time
6. noun; person who is very skilled at doing something or who knows a lot about a particular subject
7. adjective; connected with medicine
8. noun; help, less pain
9. noun; something intended to cure you when you are sick or in pain
10. verb; put in danger

IDEAS FOR... Expansion

To review the target vocabulary, ask students to close their books. Then say the sentences in random order (keeping note of the order), saying "beep" in place of the key word. Students will write the answers in their notebooks. Check the answers, the spelling, and the pronunciation as a class.

Exercise B. | Using Vocabulary

- Give some examples of different careers for the first question, or ask the class to brainstorm types of careers.

- After students write their sentences individually, have them compare answers in pairs.
- Ask volunteers to read out their sentences. Take notes of any common errors and provide feedback.

Exercise C. | Predicting

- Remind students that skimming a text means looking for the gist, or the general idea.
- Ask volunteers to read the title, subheads, and opening sentences aloud. Then have students write their ideas.
- Note: Students will check their prediction later, in exercise **A** on page 114.

track **2-03**

Ask students to read the passages. Remind them that the vocabulary definitions in the footnotes on page 113 will help them understand the reading.

Overview of the Reading

The reading passages discuss two different people who came into contact with toxins.

The first is a pianist, Leon Fleisher, who developed a crippling muscle disease that prevented him from playing. He was given the botulinum toxin, and he was able to play the piano again.

The second person was a toxicologist, Karen Wetterhahn, who was doing research on toxins. She accidentally came into contact with a drop of toxin and died a few months later.

The reading also describes how arsenic, another toxin, can be both a poison and a remedy.

Vocabulary Notes

U.S. National Institutes of Health are made up of 27 Institutes and Centers, each focusing on particular diseases or body systems. It is the largest source of funding for medical research in the world, and it funds thousands of scientists in universities and research institutions in the U.S. and around the world.

The Kennedy Center for the Arts is located in Washington, D.C. It was founded by President John F. Kennedy and named in his memory. The Kennedy Center Honors are awarded annually for exemplary lifetime achievement in the performing arts.

Dartmouth College is a prestigious private college in New Hampshire, USA.

Understanding the Reading
(page 114)

Exercise A. | Understanding the Gist

- Check students' predictions in exercise **C** on page 111.
- Have students write their sentences individually and then compare answers in pairs. Check the answers as a class.

Answer Key

1. The reading is about a pianist whose muscle disease was cured by a toxin.
2. The reading is about a scientist who died as a result of her work with toxins.

Exercise B. | Identifying Pros and Cons

- Remind students of the benefits of identifying pros and cons (see page 108).
- Draw the chart on the board and ask students to tell you the answers as you write.

Answer Key

	How it can harm	How it can help
botulinum toxin	One gram can kill 20 million people.	In small doses, it can be used to make skin look younger, to stop headaches, and to cure some diseases.
arsenic	A tenth of an ounce (2.83 grams) can cause death.	It can be used as medicine for stomach problems, asthma, and cancer.

Exercise C. | Identifying Key Details

- Remind students that key details give examples or more information about main ideas in a reading.
- Have students complete the exercise individually and then compare answers in pairs. Check answers as a class.

Answer Key

1. focal dystonia
2. control his muscles
3. a drop of dimethylmercury fell onto her hand
4. a poison
5. stomach problems
6. leukemia (a type of cancer)

Exercise D. | Understanding References

- Remind students that pronouns like *it* refer back to words (nouns or noun phrases) in an earlier part of the text. These pronoun references are used to avoid repeating information. Pronouns also help to make a text more cohesive because they make links between sentences in a paragraph.
- Do the first item together as an example. Then monitor students as they do the other items. Check the answers as a class.
- Point out the **CT Focus** box. Ask students to give some other examples using *as if.* (They were spending money as if it grew on trees.)

Answer Key   1. f 2. e 3. c 4. b

Exercise E. | Critical Thinking: Synthesizing

Encourage students to look back at the readings to review the information.

(Possible answers: 1. Catching snakes is the most dangerous because you can get bitten. 2. The Nobel Prize is named after Swedish chemist Alfred Nobel. It is a set of international awards given annually for outstanding achievement in literature, medicine, physics, chemistry, economics, and peace.

IDEAS FOR...   Expansion

Ask students to write in their journal about the kind of award they would give if they had a lot of money. What criteria would they set for someone to win the award?

Exploring Written English

45 mins *(pages 115–116)*

Exercise A. | Brainstorming

- Ask students to work in pairs to write words and/or phrases describing things that toxicologists do in their jobs. Encourage students to look back at the texts they read earlier in the unit.

- Walk around the class as students work, and help them with ideas as needed. (Possible answers: study the effects of toxins on plants, animals, and humans; study the relationship between toxins and effects; research the side effects of toxins or combinations of toxins; study the effects of different doses of toxins; determine the molecular structure of toxins; research the use of toxins to cure diseases; study the use of toxins in chemical warfare; research how to cure people who have been poisoned by toxins)

Exercise B. | Journal Writing

- Explain that this journal response will help students do the writing task in the next part of the lesson.

- Walk around as students write, and offer help or suggestions as needed.

- Ask volunteers to read out one or two ideas to the class.

Exercise C. | Analyzing

- Go over the information in the box.

- Point out the use of the comma at the end of the first clause.

- Have students write the sentences individually. Allow time for students to compare and discuss the meaning of the sentences in pairs.

- Check the answers as a class.

Answer Key

1. Although/Even though/Though just a small amount of arsenic can be deadly, it is still used to treat leukemia.

2. Although/Even though/Though snake venom is dangerous to humans, it is used in a lot of important medications.

3. Although/Even though/Though studying extinct viruses can tell us about the human species, it might bring back deadly diseases.

IDEAS FOR... **Practicing Grammar**

For exercise **C**, write additional examples on the board of sentences that can be combined using *although, even though,* or *though*. Examples:
1. She was afraid. She caught the snake.
2. He hates spiders. He studied their venom.
3. She was wearing a glove. She was poisoned.

Ask students to explain the meaning of the combined sentences in their own words.

Exercise D. | Applying

- Monitor students as they work, and help them with ideas if needed.

- Have students share their sentences with a partner or with the class.

Writing Skill: Writing a Persuasive Paragraph

Go over the information in the box. Point out how identifying pros and cons can help you to write a persuasive paragraph.

Exercise E. | Identifying Concessions

- Ask students to read through the paragraph and tell you the main idea (testing products on animals). Ask if they think the writer is for or against using animals to test products for humans. Have students scan the beginning of the paragraph to find two words that give the writer's opinion of animal testing (*cruel, unnecessary*).

- Ask students to work individually to find the sentences that make concessions and then compare answers in pairs.

- Check the answers as a class. Discuss how each concession strengthens the main argument.

Answer Key

1. Although people who support animal testing say that animals are not harmed during tests, animals usually have to live in small cages in laboratories.

2. Even though drug companies need to make their products safe for people, their products don't always have the same effect on animals and humans.

Exercise F. | Critical Thinking: Analyzing

- Walk around and monitor students as they work. Provide assistance as needed.

- Ask volunteers to read parts of their outline aloud. Check answers as a class.

Answer Key

Argument: Testing drugs on animals is cruel and unnecessary.

Supporting Idea 1: Animals are harmed.

Details: Animals usually have to live in small cages in laboratories. Animals are often badly injured during testing, and some are killed.

Supporting Idea 2: Products don't always have the same effect on animals and humans.

Details: Tests don't show how products might affect humans. Some drugs are safe for animals but not for humans.

Writing Task: Drafting *(page 117)*

Exercise A. | Planning

- Go over the steps in this exercise. Remind students that complete sentences are not necessary at this stage, and that it is more important to focus on their ideas than on grammar or spelling.

- Point out that the supporting ideas need to support and strengthen the argument.

- Walk around and monitor students as they work. Provide assistance as needed.

> **TIP** If students are having difficulty coming up with pros and cons, you could do step 1 together as a class. Draw a T-chart on the board and list the arguments in the chart.

Exercise B. | Draft 1

Walk around and monitor students as they work. Provide assistance as needed.

Writing Task: Revising
(page 118)

Exercise C. | Revising

- Remind student that the purpose of doing this activity is to help them revise their own writing later.

- Ask students to work in pairs to discuss the questions.

- Ask volunteers to explain the reasons for their choice.

Answer Key

Paragraph b is the first draft, and paragraph a is the revision.

Paragraph a introduces the main idea of the paragraph in the first sentence—the topic sentence—while paragraph b discusses expensive beauty treatments and surgeries that are not relevant.

Paragraph a uses clauses of concession that show the writer has considered the alternative point of view. There is a clause of concession in paragraph b (*Though Botox is safe, people should be happy with the way they look.*), but the ideas do not connect well.

Exercise D. | Critical Thinking: Analyzing

- Ask students to work in pairs to discuss their answers.

- Go over the answers together as a class.

Answer Key

	a	b
1.	Y	Y
2.	Y	Y
3.	Y	N
4.	Y	N
5.	Y	Y
6.	N	Y
7.	Y	Y

Exercise E. | Revising

- Explain that asking the questions in exercise **D** will help students to improve their own writing.

- Walk around and monitor students as they work. Provide assistance as needed.

Writing Task: Editing
(page 119)

> **TIP** Some students may not want to write on their partner's first draft. In this case, you can suggest that they read their partner's paragraph and use it to write an outline like the one on page 117. In most cases, if the reader can break down the information into an outline, it means the writer has produced an effective paragraph.

Exercise F. | Peer Evaluation

- Remind students that all writers need to get feedback on their writing in order to improve.

- Discuss the four steps in the evaluation process to make sure students understand what they are to do.

- The purpose of this peer evaluation is to see if each student's partner can identify the topic sentence, supporting ideas, and details that he or she intended in the first draft.

Exercise G. | Draft 2

Monitor students as they work, and provide assistance as needed.

Exercise H. | Editing Practice

- Remind students that the purpose of this exercise is to give them additional practice in editing for grammar to prepare them to do the Editing Checklist for their second draft. Focusing on grammar and punctuation at this stage prepares students to write their final draft.

- Go over the information in the box and then have students edit the five sentences.

- Check the answers by asking students to read out the correct sentences and explain the errors.

Answer Key

1. Even though she's afraid of snakes, she wants to study snake venoms.

2. Although golden poison dart frogs are very small, they **are** very deadly.

3. Even though Leon Fleisher had a serious disease, **he** can still play the piano.

4. Although a black widow's venom is deadlier than a rattlesnake's, it rarely kills humans.

5. Although there are many thousands of toxins in the wild, scientists have studied only a few hundred.

Writing Task: Editing *(page 120)*

Exercise I. | Editing Checklist

- Read the sentences in the editing checklist.

- Allow time for students to read and edit their work.

- As you monitor students' work, take notes of common errors for later feedback.

Exercise J. | Final Draft

Have students complete their third draft, and then collect their work.

TIP When giving feedback on students' written work, make sure to comment on content, ideas, and organization, as well as on grammar and mechanics.

Unit Quiz

- Students can work in groups to answer the questions.

- Encourage students to refer back to the relevant pages of the unit to find the answers.

- To do the quiz as a competition, you can have students work in teams.

Answer Key

1. Venom
2. they can hit a single target
3. they can help us find cures for diseases
4. pros, cons
5. extinct viruses
6. his muscles
7. concessions
8. persuasive

IDEAS FOR... Preventing Plagiarism

From time to time, it may be necessary to remind students of the importance of not copying material from the Internet. If your school has a written academic honesty policy, you may want to go over this with your students. Explain that in an academic setting, academic dishonesty can cause a student to fail a class.

IDEAS FOR... Journal Writing

At the end of this unit, ask students to write about a) an experience they have of being stung or bitten by an animal or an insect, or b) their opinions on animal testing.

IDEAS FOR... Further Research

Ask students to find out about other research into toxins, or to choose one poisonous animal and find out more about it. Have them write a short report about what they find out and present their reports to the class in the next lesson.

Possible Websites:

http://news.nationalgeographic.com/news/2006/09/060901-fish-venom.html

http://magma.nationalgeographic.com/ngexplorer/0911/articles/mainarticle.html

Nature's Fury

7

Academic Track
Earth Science

Academic Pathways:
Lesson A: Identifying sequence in an expository text
Lesson B: Synthesizing information from multiple texts
Lesson C: Using chronological order and transition
words to plan a paragraph
Writing a process paragraph

Unit Theme

Extreme natural events can be terrifying and amazing. Why are people fascinated by them?

Unit 7 explores the topic of extreme natural events as they relate to:

– tornadoes
– lightning

– wildfires
– earthquakes

Think and Discuss *(page 121)*

- Ask students to describe the picture. What adjectives come to mind? (Possible answers: *awesome, magnificent, majestic, stunning, terrifying, incredible*)

- Ask what students know about waterspouts and lightning (see note below).

- Discuss questions 1 and 2 as a class. Make a list on the board. You might make a word web, with the words *extreme natural events* in the center. (Possible answers: tornado, hurricane, earthquake, volcanic eruption, tsunami, monsoon, wildfire)

- Ask if students have personally experienced any extreme natural events. Share your own experiences, too.

Note: Lightning is caused by the discharge of atmospheric electricity from clouds. It is usually accompanied by thunder. A waterspout is a vertical column of spinning air over water—for example, a lake as in the photo. It is similar to a tornado and is sometimes accompanied by storms and lightning.

Exploring the Theme
(pages 122–123)

The opening spread features information about three extreme natural events: lightning, tornadoes, and wildfire.

- Ask students to look at the photos and then read the sentences in exercise **A.** (Note: They should not read the information yet.) Have students discuss the answers to exercise **A.**

- Ask students to read the information and answer the questions individually. Then discuss the questions and compare answers as a class.

Answer Key

A1. lightning 2. tornadoes 3. wildfire
B1. All three have natural causes, but wildfires are often caused by people.
2. lightning (can cause wildfires) and wildfires (can create weather systems)

> **TIP** Before beginning Lesson A, have each student make up one true/false sentence about these natural events. Ask students to work in small groups to take turns reading their sentences and having the group members answer.

IDEAS FOR... Expansion

Ask students to list any other facts they know about each of these natural events. Ask them to verify the facts and do further research for homework. They can share their findings with the class in the next lesson.

30 mins

Preparing to Read *(page 124)*

WARM-UP

The Lesson A target vocabulary is presented through a matching exercise.

Ask students to cover up the title of the article on page 125 and to look at the photograph and describe the scene. What do they think could have caused this event?

Exercise A. | Building Vocabulary

- Ask students to match the two parts of the sentences for the words that they know.
- Have students find the words they don't know in the reading and use the other words around them to guess their meanings.
- Check the answers by asking volunteers to read a sentence each.
- Point out the **Word Partners** box. Remind students that including collocations like these in their vocabulary notebooks will help them to expand their vocabulary.

> **TIP** Ask students to find other forms for the words in exercise A. (Possible answers: *(n.)* collision, *(n.)* extension, *(n.)* formation, *(n.)* occurrence, *(adj.)* regional, *(n.)* violence)

Answer Key

1. c 2. g 3. i 4. b 5. h 6. a 7. d 8. e 9. j 10. f

Exercise B. | Using Vocabulary

Ask volunteers to share their answers with the class.

> **IDEAS FOR... Expansion**
>
> You may want to bring in news articles or a video clip of a recent news story concerning a natural event. Have students ask you questions about the event and then write a short summary for homework.

Exercise C. | Brainstorming

After students complete their answers individually, have them compare answers in pairs. (Possible answers: trees fall down, roofs fly off, trailers and cars are carried away, houses are damaged or destroyed, people are killed)

Exercise D. | Predicting

- Ask students to read out the dates and places they find.
- Note: Students will check their predictions later, in exercise **A** on page 127.

Answer Key

Joplin, Missouri, April 26, 2011
United States in April 2011
April 26 to April 27, Tuscaloosa, Alabama

track **2-04**

Ask students to read the passage. Point out that the vocabulary definitions on the bottom of pages 125 and 126 will help them understand the reading.

Overview of the Reading

The passage describes tornadoes that hit Joplin, Missouri, on April 26, 2011, and Tuscaloosa, Alabama, from April 26 to 27. The article also discusses possible causes of tornadoes and describes how they form.

Understanding the Reading
(page 127)

Exercise A. | Understanding the Gist

- Check students' prediction in exercise **D** on page 124. Did they guess the general idea correctly?

Answer Key

The correct answer is item b. The 2011 date tells you that this article is about a recent tornado. Also, the tornadoes mentioned in the article all took place in the United States.

Vocabulary Notes

perfect storm (paragraph C) = a combination of circumstances that create the ideal conditions for a disaster
a monster twister (paragraph C) = a huge tornado
rotating (paragraph G) = revolving, going around in a circular motion
vertical (paragraph H) = standing or pointing straight up

Exercise B. | Identifying Main Ideas

- Have students write their answers individually and then compare answers in pairs.
- Ask volunteers to read their answers.

Answer Key

1. More violent tornadoes struck the United States in April 2011 than in any other month on record.

2. It stayed on the ground for an unusually long time.

Exercise C. | Identifying Key Details

- Encourage higher-level students to use their own words if possible. Lower-level students can copy the correct information from the text.

Answer Key

1. C, "Perfect storm" conditions occur when warm, wet air rises and collides with cold, dry air at high altitudes.

2. E, Warmer-than-normal water temperatures in the Gulf of Mexico, or a weather pattern called "La Niña," which makes air drier or wetter and causes temperatures to rise and fall.

Exercise D. | Critical Thinking: Evaluating Sources

- Discuss the difference between a quote and a paraphrase. (A quote uses the person's exact words in quotation marks; a paraphrase summarizes the person's view in different words and doesn't use quotations marks.)
- Point out the **CT Focus** box. Explain the importance of citing the source of quotes, even if they are paraphrased.

Answer Key

1. The first source (paragraph D) supports the idea that the tornado stayed on the ground a long time. The second source (paragraph E) supports the idea that experts disagree about the reason for these tornadoes.

2. The first source is described as "tornado expert Tim Samaras." The second source is described as "Russell Schneider, director of the U.S. Storm Prediction Center." The second description is more specific.

Exercise E. | Critical Thinking: Analyzing

Allow time for students to discuss the question in pairs. (Possible answer: The article says that the cause is unclear and suggests several different possibilities.)

Exercise F. | Critical Thinking: Inferring

- Have students discuss the question in pairs.
- Ask volunteers to share their ideas with the class. (Possible answer: Some people were injured. Homes and farms were destroyed or damaged. People lost their cars and other possessions.)

IDEAS FOR... Checking Comprehension

Ask these questions or write them on the board.

1. What evidence is there that the tornado was very strong? (It threw cars into the air, pulled buildings apart, and broke up pavement.)

2. Which U.S. states are mentioned in the passage, and where are they located? (Missouri—Midwest; Alabama and Georgia—South)

3. Why do experts disagree about the causes of the tornadoes? (Some think the ocean water was warmer than normal. Others think that a climate pattern, La Niña, was the cause.)

4. Find an example of figurative language in the passage. How is it effective at conveying the force of the tornado? (The tornado threw cars into the air *as if* they were toys. It helps show how strong the winds were.)

Developing Reading Skills

45 mins *(page 128)*

Reading Skill: Identifying Sequence

- Go over the information in the box.

- Point out the difference between linking words such as *first* and *next* that introduce a sentence, and conjunctions such as *before* and *after* that join clauses together.

- Ask students for some other examples of sentences that show sequence—for example, what to do in the case of a fire.

track 2-05

Exercise A. | Analyzing

- Ask students to look at the picture, to read the title, and to predict what the paragraph is about.

- Allow time for students to read and underline their answers individually.

Answer Key

If you live in a tornado region, it's important to know what to do <u>when</u> tornadoes strike. Follow these steps for what to do <u>before</u>, <u>during</u>, and <u>after</u> a tornado strikes, and you will have the best chance to stay safe. <u>First</u>, always pay attention to weather reports <u>during</u> tornado season. In addition, keep your eye on the sky. Watch for dark, greenish-colored clouds, and clouds that are close to the ground. This may mean that a tornado is coming. <u>As soon as</u> you know a tornado is about to hit, find shelter immediately if you are outdoors. If you are indoors, go to the lowest level you can, for example, to a basement. <u>Once</u> the tornado hits, stay inside for the entire time. <u>During</u> a tornado, stay away from windows, as tornadoes can cause them to break. <u>When</u> the storm is over, make sure family members are safe. Check your home and the area around it for damage. <u>Finally</u>, contact disaster relief organizations such as the American Red Cross for help with cleanup and other assistance, such as food and shelter.

Exercise B. | Identifying Sequence

- Have students discuss the questions in pairs. Explain that *over* in this context means *finished*—for example, *when the tornado is over* means *after the tornado (or storm) is finished*.

- Make a chart with three columns labeled *Before*, *During*, and *After*, and use it to check the answers with the class.

Answer Key

Before: listen to weather reports, watch the sky for dark clouds, find shelter if you're outside and go to the lowest level possible if you're inside
During: stay inside, stay away from windows
After: make sure your family is safe, check your home and the area around it for damage, contact disaster relief organizations

Exercise C. | Critical Thinking: Evaluating Sources

- Point out the **CT Focus** box. Have students identify the source line below the photo: http://www.fema.gov

- Ask what the suffix shows about the source of information in the paragraph. (The suffix shows it's a government source. Since it is a government source, it should be reliable.)

Note: FEMA stands for Federal Emergency Management Agency. It is a government department—part of the United States Department of Homeland Security—responsible for dealing with natural disasters and emergencies in the U.S.

Exercise D. | Identifying Sequence

When students have finished writing, discuss the answers as a class.

Answer Key

The sequence words are *First, Next, Then,* and *When*.

When/Once/As soon as a funnel touches the ground, it becomes a tornado.

Viewing: Lightning *(page 129)*

Overview of the Video

The video describes how lightning is formed and gives some facts about this fascinating natural phenomenon.

Vocabulary Notes

incredible = amazing, unbelievable
estimated = given an approximate quantity
extends = reaches
significant = large
vehicles = cars or other machines that carry people from place to place
deadly = likely or able to cause death

Before Viewing

Exercise A. | Using a Dictionary

- Ask students to look at the picture and describe it in their own words.

- Find out if any students know how lightning is formed and can explain it to the rest of the class.

- Have students work in pairs to discuss the words and match the definitions.

- Compare answers as a class.

Answer Key

1. expand   4. particle
2. charge   5. flash
3. volt

Exercise B. | Thinking Ahead

After pairs have discussed the T/F sentences, take a class vote on each sentence (but don't give the answers). As students watch the video, they can check their answers.

Answer Key

1. T

2. F (50–100 times a second)

3. F (Most lightning strikes are in Central Africa, the Himalayas, and South America.)

4. F (Lightning kills more people each year than hurricanes or tornadoes.)

🖵 While Viewing

Exercises A and B.

- Ask students to read the questions in exercise **B**.

- Play the video. Ask students to check their answers to exercise **B** in Before Viewing and to write short answers to questions 1–4 in exercise **B**.

Answer Key

1. Central Africa, the Himalayas, and South America

2. Lightning escapes the cloud and extends toward the ground in a branching pattern, like a tree.

3. The heat causes air around the lightning to expand, which creates the sound of thunder.

4. Find shelter inside a building or in vehicles. If caught outside, avoid high ground and isolated trees.

🖵 After Viewing

Exercise A.

- Have students discuss and compare answers.

- Play the video again and check the answers.

Exercise B. | Critical Thinking: Synthesizing

Have students work in pairs, referring back to the reading as necessary, and then discuss the answers as a class.

> ### IDEAS FOR... Checking Comprehension
>
> Replay the section of the video that describes how lightning is formed (see the Video Script on page 207). Have students take notes and write the description in their own words.
>
> *Lighter particles moving toward the top of clouds become positively charged, while heavier particles heading toward the bottom become negatively charged. In conditions where positive and negative charges grow big enough, lightning occurs between these regions.*

Preparing to Read

30 mins *(pages 130–131)*

WARM-UP

The Lesson B target vocabulary is presented in context, and students are asked to identify the part of speech and meaning of each word. Ask students what they already know about wildfires. Have them look back at page 123 to remind them of the information they read there. Ask what they know about possible ways to fight wildfires.

Exercise A. | Building Vocabulary

- Have students write their answers individually and then work in pairs to compare and discuss their answers.
- Point out the **Word Partners** box. Ask students for example sentences using these expressions (see the Ideas for Expansion box below).
- Check the answers as a class.

> **IDEAS FOR... Expansion**
>
> Write these sentence stems on the board and ask students to complete them using their own ideas.
> **1.** You need professional experience to be a good . . .
> **2.** . . . is a valuable experience.
> **3.** Past experience helps you to . . .
> **4.** . . . is a learning experience.
> **5.** You can get work experience by . . .

Answer Key

1. adjective, acceptable in a particular situation
2. verb, stop someone or something from going somewhere
3. noun, knowledge based on past events
4. adverb, happening often
5. noun, something that burns
6. noun, a particular way of doing something
7. adverb, deliberately, intentionally
8. adverb, especially
9. adjective, large enough to be important
10. noun, a plan intended to achieve a goal

Exercise B. | Using Vocabulary

- Discuss the first question as a class. Make a list of possible answers on the board. (Possible answers: Call the fire department. Pull the fire alarm. Walk calmly to the fire exit.)
- Allow time for students to write their answers to questions 2–5 individually and then discuss their answers in pairs. (Answers will vary.)

> **IDEAS FOR... Expansion**
>
> To further review the words in exercise **B**, ask students to write three additional questions using these words—for example, *What is one method for preventing house fires?* Have them ask their questions to a partner or to the class.

Exercise C. | Predicting

- Ask volunteers to read the title, subheads, and opening sentences aloud. Then have students write their ideas.
- Note: Students will check their prediction later, in exercise **A** on page 134.

 track **2-06**

Ask students to read the article. Point out the vocabulary footnotes on the bottom of page 132.

Overview of the Reading

The reading passage describes how wildfires can start, and what can be done to limit them and to fight them once they have started.

Understanding the Reading
(page 134)

Exercise A. | Understanding the Gist

Check students' predictions in exercise **C** on page 131.

Answer Key

The answer is: How to prevent wildfires from spreading. The text describes how wildfires start, but not how to prevent them starting or how to escape from them.

Exercise B. | Identifying Key Ideas

- Do the first item as an example if necessary.
- Ask students to work individually and then compare answers in pairs. Check answers as a class.

Answer Key

1. Parts of Australia, South Africa, Southern Europe, and the western regions of the United States. Paragraph: A
2. Fuel, oxygen, and a heat source. Paragraph: B
3. One strategy is to cut down trees. Another strategy is to start fires on purpose to limit the amount of fuel available for future fires. People can build fire-resistant homes. Paragraph: C

Exercise C. | Critical Thinking: Evaluating Sources

Point out the **CT Focus** box. Ask students why quotes from sources are used. (They provide support for arguments, and they help to make the argument more convincing.)

Answer Key

His comment is based on independent observation and research. It supports the idea that fire-resistant homes help to limit the spread of wildfires.

Exercise D. | Identifying Supporting Examples

- Explain that supporting examples are used to illustrate a point—in this case, to give examples of three main factors firefighters consider when fighting fires.
- Remind students to read the entire paragraph (paragraph E) before writing their answers.
- Draw the chart on the board and ask volunteers to write answers. Does the class agree?

Answer Key

Factor: shape of the land
Examples: southern-facing sides of mountains, canyons

Factor: the weather
Examples: the southern side is sunnier and drier, canyons have strong winds

Factor: the type of fuel
Examples: dry grass, plants

Exercise E. | Critical Thinking: Making Comparisons

- What two things is the writer comparing in the reading *Fighting Fire* on page 133? (fighting fires, a military campaign)
- Have students complete the sentence to answer the question in exercise **E.**

Answer Key

Possible answers:

attacks come from the air and from the ground; you have to make careful plans and evaluate the enemy; you have to develop strategies and work as a team; you have to be alert and flexible in order to stay safe.

Exercise F. | Identifying Sequence

- Have students underline the sequencing words and then number the sentences in the correct order.
- Check the answers as a class.

Answer Key

The sequencing words: first, then, while, As soon as, At the same time

a. 3 **b.** 1 **c.** 3 **d.** 2 **e.** 2

Exercise G. | Critical Thinking: Synthesizing

Compare answers as a class.

Answer Key

Possible answers:

1. Tornadoes are caused by the collision of warm, wet air and cold, dry air at high altitudes. Wildfires usually occur in areas where wet weather is followed by long, hot, dry weather.
2. Tornadoes cannot be predicted or prevented. Wildfires can sometimes be predicted, and they can be controlled and prevented to some extent.

Exploring Written English
(pages 135–136)

45 mins

Exercise A. | Brainstorming

Help students to brainstorm some examples of different processes by giving a few examples. (Possible answers: How rain is formed, how hurricanes are formed, what to do in case of a flood warning, what to do in an earthquake)

Exercise B. | Journal Writing

Allow time for students to work individually. Walk around as students write, and offer help or suggestions as needed.

Exercise C. | Analyzing

- Go over the information in the box. Remind students of words that show sequence.
- Have students complete the sentences.

Answer Key

1. Move 2. dig 3. collides

IDEAS FOR...   Practicing Grammar

Ask students to think of a situation where they gave or were given some instructions using the imperative. Have students write one sentence and read it aloud. The other students try to guess the situation—for example, *Please turn off your cell phones.* Situation: at a concert; in an airplane

---

Exercise D. | Applying

- Monitor students as they work, and help them with ideas if needed.
- Have students share their sentences with a partner or the class.

Writing Skill: Organizing a Process Paragraph

Go over the information in the box. Review the transition words and phrases on page 128 if necessary.

Exercise E. | Sequencing

- Ask students to read through the sentences and tell you the main idea of the paragraph (how to avoid danger when a wildfire occurs).
- Have students work individually to underline the transition words and phrases that show order. Then check answers as a class. (See Answer Key.)

- Check the correct sequence of sentences before students start to write.

Answer Key   3, 5, 2, 1, 4

Answer Key

Wildfires move quickly and are extremely dangerous, but you can avoid danger if you follow these steps. If a fire is approaching your home, <u>first</u> go outside and move any items that can act as fuel for the fire, such as dead plants. <u>Then</u> go back inside and close all windows, doors, and other openings. This helps prevent the fire from moving easily through the house. <u>After that</u>, turn off any of your home energy sources that can act as fuel, such as natural gas. <u>Then</u> fill large containers such as garbage cans and bathtubs with water. This will slow down the fire. <u>Finally</u>, leave the area as quickly as possible. Do not return home <u>until</u> it is safe. If you follow these steps, you will have the best chances for staying safe if a wildfire occurs.

Writing Task: Drafting
(page 137)

Exercise A. | Planning

- Go over the steps. Remind students that complete sentences are not necessary and that it is more important to focus on their ideas than on grammar or spelling.
- Walk around and monitor students as they work. Provide assistance as needed.

TIP   If students are having difficulty coming up with details, ask questions starting with *How* or *Why* to help them—for example, *Why do you need to go inside?*

Exercise B. | Draft 1

Walk around and monitor students as they work. Provide assistance as needed.

Writing Task: Revising

(page 138)

Exercise C. | Analyzing

- Remind students that doing this activity will help them to revise their own writing.
- Ask students to work in pairs to discuss the questions.
- Ask volunteers to explain the reasons for their choice.

Answer Key

Paragraph b is the first draft, and paragraph a is the revision.

The topic sentence in paragraph a expresses the main idea more accurately. Paragraph a presents the steps in chronological order. Paragraph b doesn't use transition words and phrases to show order. Paragraph a has two additional steps. (*Then drop to the ground. Be careful opening cupboards.*) It also gives more details than paragraph b. (*You will be safer if you move as little as possible.*)

Exercise D. | Critical Thinking: Analyzing

- Ask students to work in pairs to discuss their answers.
- Go over the answers together as a class.

Answer Key

	a	b
1.	Y	Y
2.	Y	N
3.	Y	N
4.	Y	N
5.	Y	Y
6.	Y	Y

Exercise E. | Revising

- Remind students that asking the questions in exercise **D** will help them to improve their own writing.
- Walk around and monitor students as they work. Provide assistance as needed.

Writing Task: Editing

(page 139)

Exercise F. | Peer Evaluation

- Discuss the four steps in the evaluation process to make sure students understand what they are to do.
- The purpose of this peer evaluation is to see if each student's partner can identify the steps or events that he or she intended in the first draft.

TIP Alternatively, students might underline and number the steps and draw a wavy line under the details. You could also have students suggest additional details for their partner to use in draft 2.

Exercise G. | Draft 2

Monitor students as they work, and provide assistance as needed.

Exercise H. | Editing Practice

- Go over the information, and then have students edit the five sentences.
- Write the sentences on the board and ask volunteers to make the corrections. Ask a volunteer to explain each of the errors.

Answer Key

1. Most earthquake injuries **happen** when people go outside before the quake is over.
2. Before a tornado hits, **listen** carefully to weather reports.
3. When lighting **strikes**, move indoors as quickly as possible.
4. **Find** the lowest area in a building when a tornado is about to hit.
5. A firefighter **tries** to remove fuel in the fire's path, such as dead trees and plants.

Writing Task: Editing

(page 140)

Exercise I. | Editing Checklist

- Read the sentences in the editing checklist.
- Allow time for students to read and edit their work.
- As you monitor students' work, you may take notes on common errors for later feedback.

Exercise J. | Final Draft

Have students complete their third draft, and then collect their work.

TIP When giving feedback on students' written work, make sure to balance positive comments with suggestions for improvement.

Unit Quiz

- Students can work in groups to answer the questions.
- Encourage students to refer back to the relevant pages of the unit to find the answers.
- To do the quiz as a competition, you can have students work in teams.

Answer Key

1. twister
2. Tornado Alley
3. collides
4. at the same time
5. flash
6. Fuel
7. on purpose
8. order

IDEAS FOR... Reviewing Vocabulary

- Select 25 words from this unit. Write each word on a separate slip of paper. Put the slips in a paper bag.
- Divide the class into five groups. Each group will select five words from the bag and then work together as a group to write a paragraph containing these five words. They will leave blanks for the target words. Then they will exchange paragraphs with another group and write the answers in their notebooks.
- All paragraphs can be passed around so that every group gets to read all the paragraphs.

IDEAS FOR... Journal Writing

At the end of this unit, ask students to write about a) an extreme weather event that has happened recently in your region; b) a first-hand account of an extreme weather event, either fictional or true; or c) what they would do to help limit or prevent injury and damage from tornadoes, earthquakes, or another natural disaster.

IDEAS FOR... Further Research

Ask students to research one of these topics and present their reports to the class in the next lesson:

a. current scientific opinions about the reasons for the increase in extreme weather events

b. the controversy about using controlled fires to prevent wildfires

c. information about another type of extreme weather event—for example, hurricanes, monsoons, hailstones, drought

Building Wonders

Academic Track
**Anthropology
and Sociology/
Archaeology**

Academic Pathways:
Lesson A: Scanning for specific information
Lesson B: Reading a comparison text
Lesson C: Using a Venn diagram to plan a paragraph
Writing a comparison paragraph

Unit Theme

What does architecture tell us about our culture and the values of our civilization? How does architecture affect our daily lives?

Unit 8 explores the topic of architecture as it relates to:

– the La Sagrada Família Cathedral
– the sculptures of Rapa Nui
– the ancient pyramids of Egypt
– Göbekli Tepe and Chichén Itzá

Think and Discuss *(page 141)*

- Ask students to describe the picture. (Useful words: *construction site, scaffolding, laborers, construction workers, concrete, cement*) Ask what the picture brings to mind. (Possible answers: a beehive, an ants' nest)

- Discuss questions 1 and 2 as a class. Make a list of buildings on the board for each question. (Possible answers for question 2: the Taj Mahal in India, Notre Dame Cathedral in France, the Guggenheim Museum in Bilbao, Spain, the Burj Al Arab Tower in Dubai, the Shard Building in London)

- Ask students their opinion of architecture in their city or region. What is special about it? What do they like or dislike about modern architecture?

Exploring the Theme
(pages 142–143)

The opening spread features a picture of work being done on the monument of Mount Rushmore in South Dakota, in the U.S.

- Ask students to look at the picture and read the caption. Ask if they know what other faces are carved on this monument.

- Discuss the answers to question 1 and make a list on the board. Then ask students to read the text. (Possible answers: to commemorate a person or an event, to symbolize power and wealth, to attract visitors, to display technical progress)

- Discuss question 2 and make a list on the board. (Possible answers: the Eiffel Tower in Paris, the Pyramids in Egypt, the Statue of Liberty in New York City, the Obelisk of Byzantine in Istanbul, Turkey)

- Discuss question 3 and ask students to explain what would make them want to visit one of these monuments.

Note: Mount Rushmore is a mountain in South Dakota on which is carved the heads of four presidents of the United States: George Washington (president from 1789 to 1797), Thomas Jefferson (from 1801 to 1809), Theodore Roosevelt (from 1901 to 1909), and Abraham Lincoln (from 1861 to 1865).

The designer and sculptor was Gutzon Borglum. Along with about 400 workers, he carved the 60-foot heads from the bare rock. The monument was completed in 1941.

George Washington was chosen because he led the nation to democracy; Thomas Jefferson because he wrote the Declaration of Independence; Abraham Lincoln because he abolished slavery in the U.S.; and Theodore Roosevelt because he promoted the construction of the Panama Canal as well as the causes of conservation and business.

> **IDEAS FOR... Expansion**
>
> Ask students to write a paragraph in their journal about a building or monument they would like to visit and explain why.

Preparing to Read *(page 144)*

30 mins

WARM-UP

The Lesson A target vocabulary is presented through an exercise where students are asked to match words with their definitions.

Ask students if they are familiar with any famous cathedrals (for example, Notre Dame Cathedral in France or Canterbury Cathedral in England) and what they know about them. When were they built? How does the architectural style reflect their purpose?

Exercise A. | Building Vocabulary

- Ask students to read the words and definitions and match up any that they already know.

- Have students find the words they don't know in the reading and use the other words around them to guess their meanings.

- Check the answers by asking a question about each word. For example:

  T: What's an architect?

  S: It's a person who plans or designs buildings.

- Point out the **Word Partners** box. Remind students to include these phrases in their vocabulary notebooks.

TIP Ask students to give other word forms for the words in exercise A. (Possible answers: *(adj.)* architectural; *(n.)* commitment; *(n.)* illustration; *(v.)* inspire; *(n.)* succession; *(n.)* sculptor; *(adj.)* structural; *(adj.)* stylistic; *(adj.)* symbolic, *(v.)* symbolize; *(adj.)* thematic)

Answer Key

1. i 2. j 3. b 4. d 5. h 6. c 7. f 8. g 9. a 10. e

Exercise B. | Using Vocabulary

Ask volunteers to share their answers with the class.

> **IDEAS FOR... Expansion**
>
> You may want to assign question 2 or 3 in exercise **B** as a journal task for homework.

Exercise C. | Brainstorming

After students complete their answers individually, have them compare answers in pairs. (Possible answers: The ceiling is painted to look like the sky at night. The walls are decorated with flowers. The windows are shaped like tree leaves or branches.)

Exercise D. | Predicting

- Remind students that predicting will help them to understand the passage when they start to read it in detail.

- Ask students to read out the dates and places they find.

- Note: Students will check their predictions later, in exercise **A** on page 149.

track **2-07**

Ask students to read the passage.

- Note that the reading is in two parts. The first part, *Unfinished Masterpiece*, is on pages 145 and 148. (If you use the audio program, this part is first on track 2-07.) The second part, *Barcelona's Natural Wonder*, is on pages 146 and 147. (This part appears next on track 2-07.)

- Point out the footnotes on pages 145 and 148, which will help students understand the reading.

Overview of the Reading

The passage is about the famous Spanish architect Antoní Gaudí and his most famous building, La Sagrada Família Cathedral in Barcelona, which was unfinished at the time of his death in 1926. Construction work on this architectural wonder continues to this day.

Gaudí created many buildings in Barcelona, but the most famous is the unfinished La Sagrada Família. It has sparked fierce controversy among the inhabitants of Barcelona—about the design, which was very unconventional for its time; about the cost; and then after Gaudí's death, about how best to complete the project in the way he had intended.

On June 7, 1926, Gaudí was run over by a tram at a busy intersection in Barcelona. He was so poorly dressed that the taxi drivers refused to take him to the hospital, thinking that he was a beggar. On the day of his funeral, half of Barcelona dressed in black out of respect for him. His body was buried in the crypt of La Sagrada Família, where he had worked for the last 43 years of his life.

Understanding the Reading
(page 149)

Exercise A. | Understanding the Gist

Check students' predictions in exercise **D** on page 144. Did they guess the general ideas correctly?

Answer Key

1. an architect

2. a cathedral

3. It was inspired by nature.

Vocabulary Notes

La Sagrada Família (paragraph A) = the Holy Family
natural wonders (paragraph B) = for example, the landscape, hills, mountains, rock formations
honor (paragraph C) = show love and respect
wildlife (paragraph D) = animals and other living things that live in the wild
turtle and tortoise (paragraph D) = small animals with a shell covering their body
carving (paragraph D) = picture or sculpture created by cutting stone or wood
survived (paragraph E) = were not lost or destroyed
timeless (paragraph F) = so good or beautiful that it cannot be affected by changes in society or fashion

Exercise B. | Identifying Main Ideas

- Explain that students should identify the main points of each paragraph and summarize them.

- Invite volunteers to read their answers. Ask the class if they agree.

Answer Key

1. He was inspired by nature and thought the best way to honor God was by designing buildings based on natural forms.

2. The inside of the building feels like a forest because the pillars are shaped like trees. The outside is decorated with shapes of animals and birds.

3. He made three-dimensional models of his plans.

Exercise C. | Identifying Supporting Details

- Remind students that a chart is a useful way to organize detailed information.

- Allow students time to complete the exercise individually or in pairs.

- Check answers as a class.

Answer Key

Inside:
pillars . . . trees
windows . . . sea algae
wall decorations . . . vines
spiral stairway . . . snail

Outside:
towers . . . trees
tower tops . . . crystals, grains, and grasses
sculptures . . . animals and birds

Exercise D. | Critical Thinking: Reflection

Check answers as a class. (Answers will vary for questions 1 and 3. For question 2, Gaudí probably meant that God was his client and that God was not in a hurry to see the cathedral completed.)

IDEAS FOR... Checking Comprehension

Ask these questions or write them on the board. Note that they require students to make some inferences based on information in the text and their own general knowledge.

1. Why do you think the building is unfinished? (It has taken a lot of time and money to carry out these very detailed and intricate plans; also, building was interrupted by the Spanish Civil War.)

2. Why do you think it was important for the city to have a cathedral? (To show the city's importance, to provide a place of worship for people of the region, to express their love of God by creating something beautiful)

3. How do you think the style of this building differs from other church styles? (It has curved lines instead of straight lines; the interior is highly decorated in vivid colors; it has a cluster of spires around one large central spire instead of just one spire.)

4. Why do you think the building is called *a natural wonder*? (Although it is man-made, its design is inspired by nature and the building looks almost organic.)

Developing Reading Skills
(page 150)

45 mins

Reading Skill: Scanning for Specific Information

- Go over the information in the box.
- Point out the **Strategy** box. Practice looking for paraphrases by asking students to look for a paraphrase of each of the following words in the reading passage on pages 145–148:

  buildings, paragraph B (structures)
  tried out, paragraph C (experimented with)
  sculptures, paragraph D (carvings)
  were not lost, paragraph E (survived)

track **2-08**

Exercise A. | Scanning for Details

- Ask students to look at the picture and say what they know about the moai (large, carved statues) of Rapa Nui. If they don't know anything, ask them to describe the sculpture in the picture and say what they think it was created for.
- Allow time for students to read the text.
- After checking the answers as a class, have students read the text again and work in pairs to ask and answer questions about it. You might ask students to find out more about these statues for homework.

Note: The moai are large stone figures of humans with huge heads that were built between the years 1250 and 1500 on the Polynesian island of Rapa Nui. (Rapa Nui is the Polynesian name; the European name is Easter Island.) There are 887 statues altogether, and they are thought to represent sacred ancestors. The tallest moai was almost 33 feet (10 meters) high and weighed 82 tons. It is not known exactly how the moai were moved across the island from the quarry to the hilltops. It is possible that wooden sledges or rollers were used. When Dutch explorers landed on the island in 1772, all the trees had disappeared.

Answer Key

1. 2,300 miles (3,700 kilometers)
2. AD 800
3. the Polynesian islands
4. 13 feet (4 meters) tall, 14 tons

Exercise B. | Scanning for Details

When students have finished writing, discuss the answers as a class.

Answer Key

1. 1910 (Paragraph B)
2. Mark Burry (Paragraph E)
3. 2026 (Paragraph G)
4. Some were lost. (Paragraph E)

IDEAS FOR... Expansion

Ask students to work in pairs to take turns coming up with some other items in the text that could be found by scanning.
For example:
Student A: the name of a region
Student B: Catalonia
Student B: the name of a city
Student A: Barcelona
Student A: three types of animals
Student B: a turtle, a tortoise, a snail

Viewing: The Pyramids of Giza *(page 151)*

Overview of the Video

The video gives information about the ancient pyramids in Giza, Egypt, and explains why archaeologists are still studying them today.

The video describes three pyramids:

1. Pyramid of Khufu
2. Pyramid of Khafre
3. Pyramid of Menkaure

Before Viewing

Exercise A. | Brainstorming

- Ask students to look at the picture and say what they already know about the pyramids of ancient Egypt.
- Note: Do not check the answers yet as students will check their answers when they watch the video.

Answer Key

places for dead bodies

Exercise B. | Using a Dictionary

Have students check the answers in pairs, or check them as a class.

Answer Key

1. pharaoh
2. the afterlife
3. tombs
4. possessions
5. archaeologist

While Viewing

Exercises A and B.

- Ask students to read the questions in exercise **B**.
- Play the video. Ask students to check their answers to the Brainstorming exercise in Before Viewing and to write short answers to questions 1–4 in exercise **B**.

Answer Key

1. 4,000 years
2. over two million stone blocks, each weighing almost 2,300 kilograms
3. 20 years
4. It has the head of a man. Experts think it represents Pharaoh Khafre himself.

After Viewing

Exercise A.

- Have students discuss and compare answers.
- Play the video again and check the answers.

Exercise B. | Critical Thinking: Synthesizing

Have students work in pairs and compare the structures, referring back to the readings as needed. Discuss the answers as a class.

IDEAS FOR... Checking Comprehension

1. Ask: *What was the main purpose of the pyramids?* (They were tombs for the pharaohs. They were built to guard the pharaoh's body and possessions, and to transport him into the afterlife.)
2. Write the names of the three pyramids on the board. Play the video again and ask students to take notes on any additional details about each of these pyramids. (Pyramid of Khufu: largest, oldest, 140 meters tall, thousands of workers built it, Pharaoh Khufu ruled 4,500 years ago; Pyramid of Khafre: made for Khufu's son, guarded by a statue of the Sphinx which is 70 meters long and combines the body of a lion and the head of a man; Pyramid of Menkaure: smallest, made for Khafre's son, many surrounding tombs and temples have not been studied yet)
3. Ask: *What is still mysterious about the pyramids and what do archaeologists still want to find out?* (How were they built? Why were they designed in this way? Why were they so important to ancient Egyptians? What role did they play in everyday life? Who does the Sphinx really represent?)

Preparing to Read

30 mins *(pages 152–153)*

WARM-UP

The Lesson B target vocabulary is presented in context; students are asked to choose the correct meaning and identify the part of speech as the word is used in the sentence.

Ask students what they already know about stone circles. They may have heard of Stonehenge in England, for example. What were they created for? Why are they special? Ask what students know about the pyramids in Mexico. Who built them? What were they created for?

Exercise A. | Building Vocabulary

• Allow time for students to write their answers individually and then compare answers in pairs.

• Point out the **Word Link** box. Ask students for other examples of words with *trans*—for example, *transform, transition, transplant, transmit.*

Answer Key

1. b, noun	**6.** b, verb
2. a, verb	**7.** b, verb
3. b, verb	**8.** a, noun
4. a, verb	**9.** b, noun
5. a, verb	**10.** a, verb

Exercise B. | Using Vocabulary

• Discuss the first question as a class. Make a list of possible answers.

• Allow time for students to write their answers individually and then discuss them in pairs. (Possible answers: 1. anger, danger, good luck, happiness, fire 2. climate change, the economic crisis, world poverty 3. train, truck, ship, plane 4. a treehouse, a model car or airplane 5. Answers will vary.)

> **IDEAS FOR...** Expansion
>
> To review the words in exercise **B**, ask students to make additional questions with these words, using more than one vocabulary word in each question if possible. For example, *What is one **site** that archaeologists have **excavated**?* They can ask their questions to a partner or to the class.

Exercise C. | Scanning/Previewing

• Ask students to scan the article for names of places.

• Note: Students will check their answers later, in exercise **A** on page 156.

track **2-09**

Ask students to read the passage. Point out that the vocabulary definitions in the footnotes on the bottom of page 155 will help them as they read.

Overview of the Reading

The reading passage describes two amazing structures. Göbekli Tepe is a stone circle in Turkey. Chichén Itzá is a Mayan temple in Mexico.

Understanding the Reading
(page 156)

Exercise A. | Understanding the Gist

Check students' predictions in exercise **C** on page 153.

Answer Key

1. ancient structures
2. Turkey, Mexico

Vocabulary Notes

stepped (paragraph E) = with a series of descending steps like a staircase
advanced (paragraph G) = sophisticated, complex

IDEAS FOR... Expansion

As an alternative way to do this reading, divide the class into two groups. Give each group one of the reading passages. Then pair up students from each group to exchange and compare their information.

Exercise B. | Scanning for Specific Information

- Point out that students may have to paraphrase information from the text.
- Draw the chart on the board and ask volunteers to write the answers.

Answer Key

Göbekli Tepe: 11,590 BC, by carving pillars from stone and transporting them to the site

Chichén Itzá: AD 750–1200, by creating a base of carved stone and adding levels to make it higher

Exercise C. | Critical Thinking: Evaluating Arguments

- Point out the importance of evaluating arguments presented in the text. In this case, archaeologists are not sure about the original purpose of these sites, so they have to make inferences based on evidence they find.
- Point out that there are two possible answers for each point for Chichén Itzá.

Answer Key

Göbekli Tepe
Purpose: a holy meeting place

Evidence: The T-shaped pillars represent human beings. They face the center of the circle and perhaps represent a religious ritual.

Chichén Itzá
Purpose: a religious site, a place to make sacrifices to a god; a place to view Venus and other planets

Evidence: Bones, jewelry, and other objects that people wore when they were sacrificed have been found. Mayans were excellent astronomers.

Exercise D. | Critical Thinking: Analyzing Similarities and Differences

- Remind students that a Venn diagram is a useful way to organize similarities and differences.
- Point out the **CT Focus** box. Ask students to list possible topics for comparing these two sites. (Possible answers: age, location, purpose, method of construction, materials used, length of time needed)
- Draw the chart on the board and ask the class to tell you what to write in it.

Answer Key

Göbekli Tepe: located in Turkey, built 11,590 BC, people lived in small nomadic groups

Middle area: used for rituals, made from carved stone, required hundreds of workers

Chichén Itzá: located in Mexico, built AD 750–1200, used for astronomy, bones and jewelry found at the site, people lived in cities

Exercise E. | Critical Thinking: Synthesizing

- You might ask students to complete a similar Venn diagram about their two chosen structures.
- Ask volunteers to summarize the differences and similarities for the class.

IDEAS FOR... Checking Comprehension

Divide the class into two groups. Ask each student to prepare a question about one of the reading passages (they should work as a group so that no questions are repeated). Then ask all students to close their books. Each student will ask someone in the other group his or her question. You might organize this as a competition, with points for correct answers.

Exploring Written English

45 mins *(pages 157–158)*

Exercise A. | Brainstorming

Ask students to work in pairs to write words or phrases in their books. Help them with ideas if needed.

Exercise B. | Journal Writing

Allow time for students to work individually. Offer students help or suggestions as needed.

Exercise C. | Analyzing

- Go over the information in the box.
- Ask students for further examples of adjectives that could be used to describe buildings, and review how the comparative is formed. (Possible answers: big, small, impressive, elegant, ancient, modern, beautiful, ugly)
- Ask students to rephrase each example in the box as follows:

  Stonehenge is not as old as Göbekli Tepe.

  The design of St. Patrick's Cathedral is not as complex as the design of La Sagrada Família.

  The Tokyo Sky Tree is taller than the Empire State Building.

- Have students complete the sentences.

Answer Key

1. taller
2. not as traditional as
3. as long as

IDEAS FOR... Practicing Grammar

Ask students to write three sentences about buildings in their town or region. Then have students exchange their sentences with another student and paraphrase them using alternative comparative structures.

Exercise D. | Applying

- Monitor students as they work, and help them with ideas if needed.
- Have students share their sentences with a partner or the class.

Writing Skill: Writing a Comparison Paragraph

- Go over the information in the box. Review the transition words in the box. Which can be used at the beginning of a sentence? Which can be used within a sentence?
- Summarize the main points in the box as numbered steps on the board.

  1. Choose the topic.
  2. Think of three points.
  3. Think of two details for each point.
  4. Use transition words and phrases.

Exercise E. | Critical Thinking: Analyzing

- Point out the **CT Focus** box. Discuss the advantages of using graphic organizers to aid organization and memory.
- Ask students to read the paragraph and complete the notes.
- Draw the Venn diagram on the board. Ask volunteers to write their answers.

Answer Key

The Grant Library: built in 1890, classical style with marble columns like a Greek temple, open 24 hours a day

Middle area: used for student research, part of BCU college campus, both have books available for students to use, both are libraries

The Barrett Library: built in early 20th century, craftsman style, made of wood, library and museum, open 7 hours a day

Exercise F. | Critical Thinking: Analyzing

- Discuss the answers to the questions.
- Ask students to find examples of comparative adjectives and transition words in the paragraph and circle them.

Answer Key

1. style and purpose

2. & 3. The Grant Library and the Barrett Library are (both) important resources for BCU students, but there are some (differences) between the two structures. First, the buildings have very (different) styles. The Grant Library, built in 1890, is (older) than the Barrett Library. It was built in the classical style. For example, there are tall marble columns at the entrance, which make the library look like a Greek temple. The Barrett Library, (on the other hand,) has a (newer) design. It was built in the early 20th century in the craftsman style. It is made entirely of wood and blends in with the natural environment. The purposes of the two libraries are (also) different. Students can do research at (both) places, but the Barrett Library is also a museum, so it's open only seven hours a day. The Grant Library, however, is open 24 hours a day. So students can study there for a (longer) time. The two buildings have (different) styles and purposes, (but both) are excellent examples of the variety of architectural styles on the BCU campus.

Writing Task: Drafting
(page 159)

TIP To introduce this exercise, you may want to bring in pictures of famous buildings to give students ideas and help them to think about ways to compare buildings.

Exercise A. | Planning

- Go over the steps. Remind students that complete sentences are not necessary at this stage and that it is more important to focus on their ideas than on grammar or spelling.

- Walk around and monitor students as they work. Provide assistance as needed.

- Ask three or four volunteers to share their topic sentence, one of their points, and a supporting detail with the class.

Exercise B. | Draft 1

Walk around and monitor students as they work. Provide assistance as needed.

Writing Task: Revising
(page 160)

Exercise C. | Analyzing

- Ask students to look at the pictures and say what they know about these two bridges.

- Ask students to work in pairs to discuss the questions.

- Ask volunteers to explain the reasons for their choice.

- Point out the **Strategy** box. Ask students to check the pronouns in these paragraphs. Ask them to think about whether or not it is always clear to the reader what the pronouns refer to.

Answer Key

Paragraph a is the first draft, and paragraph b is the revision.

Paragraph b is more clearly organized. It describes four points of comparison (design, length, age, and purpose), does not include irrelevant information, includes transition words, and has a good concluding sentence that summarizes the paragraph.

Paragraph a mentions only two points of comparison, includes irrelevant information such as the origin of the name of the Golden Gate Bridge, does not include many transition words, and does not have a concluding sentence.

Exercise D. | Critical Thinking: Analyzing

- Ask students to work in pairs to discuss their answers.

- Go over the answers together as a class.

Answer Key

	a	b
1.	N	Y
2.	Y	Y
3.	Y	Y
4.	N	Y
5.	N	Y
6.	N	Y

Exercise E. | Revising

Walk around and monitor students as they work. Provide assistance as needed.

Writing Task: Editing

(page 161)

Exercise F. | Peer Evaluation

Go over the five steps in the evaluation process to make sure students understand what they are to do.

Exercise G. | Draft 2

Monitor students as they work, and provide assistance as needed.

Exercise H. | Editing Practice

- Go over the information in the box and then have students edit the five sentences.
- Write the sentences on the board and ask volunteers to correct them and explain the errors.

Answer Key

1. The Chelsea Hotel is ~~more~~ **smaller** than Casa Mila.

2. La Sagrada Família is **more attractive** than St. Mary's Cathedral.

3. The construction of the Morrison Library was more **expensive** than the construction of the Barrett Library.

4. The Tokyo Sky Tree is not **as** tall as the Burj Khalifa in Dubai.

5. The carvings on the columns in La Sagrada Família are not as ancient **as** the columns of Göbekli Tepe.

Writing Task: Editing

(page 162)

Exercise I. | Editing Checklist

- Read the sentences in the editing checklist. Allow time for students to read and edit their work.
- As you monitor students' work, you may want to take notes on common errors for later feedback.

Exercise J. | Final Draft

Have students complete their third draft, and then collect their work.

Unit Quiz

- Students can work in groups to answer the questions.
- Encourage students to refer back to the relevant pages of the unit to find the answers.
- To do the quiz as a competition, you can have students work in teams.

Answer Key

1. monument	5. tombs
2. theme	6. temple
3. nature	7. comparisons
4. details	8. both differences and similarities

IDEAS FOR... **Reviewing Grammar**

Use students' homework to select around 20 sentences that contain examples of common errors. Write the sentences on the board. Ask students to work in teams to correct them. The team with the most correct sentences wins.

IDEAS FOR... **Journal Writing**

At the end of this unit, ask students to write about a) their favorite building; b) what they feel is important about architecture today; or c) a famous building that they have visited and what the experience was like.

IDEAS FOR... **Further Research**

Ask students to research one of these topics and present their reports to the class in the next lesson:
a) a famous building or monument;
b) one type of architectural style; or
c) an ancient structure that remains mysterious today.

Form and Function

Academic Track
Life Science

Academic Pathways:
Lesson A: Distinguishing facts from theories
Lesson B: Synthesizing information from related texts
Lesson C: Paraphrasing and summarizing
           Writing a summary

Unit Theme

How did features of the natural world emerge and develop? How do people use ideas from nature to invent new things?

Unit 9 explores the topic of form and function in nature as it relates to:

– the evolution of feathers
– animal adaptations

– the relationship between dinosaurs and birds
– biomimetics

Think and Discuss *(page 163)*

- Ask students to describe the picture. (Useful words: *wings, beak, claws, feathers, beat, flap, dive, hover, catch, prey*) What does it tell us about nature? (Possible answers: It is a fight for survival. Animals are dependent on each other for food. Animals are part of the food chain.)

- Discuss question 1. (Possible answers: to keep warm, for protection)

- You might have students discuss question 2 in pairs to get a wider a range of possible answers.

Answer Key

Possible answers:

1. Polar bears have fur to keep them warm. Elephants have skin that keeps them cool by evaporating moisture easily. Snakes have scales that help them to move along the ground.

2. Velcro (inspired by a plant), sonar (inspired by the use of echolocation by bats and dolphins), airplane design (based on wings of birds), bionic car (based on the design of fish), self-cooling buildings (based on design of termite mounds); churches (Gaudí's La Sagrada Família, in Unit 8); swim fins

Exploring the Theme *(pages 164–165)*

15 mins

- Ask students to look at the pictures and say what they know about how snakes and birds have adapted to their environment. For example, snakes are described as cold-blooded because their body temperature changes according to their environment, unlike humans who have a constant body temperature.

- For question 3, brainstorm examples and classify them as behavioral or physical.

Answer Key

1. An example of a physical adaptation is plants that have adapted to living in the desert by storing water in their stems. An example of a behavioral adaptation is gray whales that give birth in warm water, but travel to cold water for food.

2. The scarlet king snake and the steppe eagle chicks show a physical adaptation. The hummingbird shows a behavioral adaptation.

3. Another example of behavioral adaptation is nocturnal animals such as bats. They can avoid competition from birds, and it's easier to hide from predators. An example of a physical adaptation is the panda, which has developed a special thumb that helps it eat bamboo.

IDEAS FOR... Expansion

Ask students to choose an animal and do some research on how it has adapted. They can bring in pictures and present the information in class.

Preparing to Read *(page 166)*

30 mins

WARM-UP

The Lesson A target vocabulary is presented through a sentence-completion exercise in which the words are given in context.

Ask students what they know about birds. You could draw a bird on the board and ask students to label each part (wing, beak, claw, feathers, crest).

Ask them to describe how birds are different from mammals or reptiles. Can they swim? What do they eat? Where do they live? You may want to choose two different birds—for example, a heron and an eagle—and compare them.

Exercise A. | Building Vocabulary

- Ask students to read the words and circle those that they are not sure about. Then ask them to find the unfamiliar words in the passage and use the context to try to guess their meaning.

- Point out the **Word Partners** box. Ask for some other collocations with the word *theory*—for example, *economic theory, educational theory.*

TIP After checking the answers, ask students to give other word forms for these words. (Possible answers: *(n.)* evolution, *(n.)* flexibility, *(v.)* fossilize, *(v.)* insulate, *(n.)* speculation, *(adj.)* theoretical)

Answer Key

1. speculate	**6.** display
2. Insulation	**7.** Evidence
3. fossil	**8.** evolve
4. theory	**9.** flexible
5. layer	**10.** primitive

Exercise B. | Using Vocabulary

Ask volunteers to share their answers with the class.

Answer Key

Possible answers:

1. a paper book cover, a plastic bag, a leather glove or shoe

2. fingerprints, DNA material at the crime scene, witness reports

3. Darwin's theory of evolution, Einstein's theory of relativity

Exercise C. | Brainstorming

After students complete their answers individually, have them compare answers in pairs. (Possible answers: to attract a mate, to disguise themselves, or to blend in with their environment so they can catch prey more easily)

Exercise D. | Predicting

- Point out the **Strategy** box. Ask volunteers to read the title and subheads aloud.

- Note: Students will check their predictions later, in exercise **A** on page 169.

track **2-10** Ask students to read the passage on pages 167–168. Point out that the vocabulary definitions on the bottom of these pages will help them understand the reading.

Overview of the Reading

The passage is about three possible reasons for the development of feathers in birds: insulation (to provide warmth), attraction (to attract a mate), and flight.

Understanding the Reading
(page 169)

Exercise A. | Understanding the Gist

Check students' prediction in exercise **D** on page 166. Did they guess the general idea correctly?

Answer Key

b. three possible purposes of feathers

Vocabulary Notes

young (paragraph B) = babies
spread (paragraph B) = covering
the opposite sex (paragraph C) = for males, females; for females, males
at an angle (paragraph E) = not straight
relatives (paragraph F) = family members
clue (paragraph F) = evidence that helps to solve a problem
moveable (paragraph G) = can be moved
fold its arms (paragraph G) = bring its arms close to its body

Exercise B. | Identifying Main Ideas

- If students have difficulty, prompt them to look at the subheads.
- Check answers as a class.

Answer Key

Purpose:

1. insulation (to provide warmth) **2.** attraction (to attract a mate) **3.** flight

Exercise C. | Identifying Supporting Details

- Go over the instructions and point out that the examples should relate to modern-day facts, whereas the evidence should relate to fossils.
- Have students complete the chart individually and then compare answers in pairs. Check answers as a class.

Answer Key

1. Purpose: insulation
Examples: Young birds have a layer of soft feathers that keep their bodies warm.
Evidence: Paleontologists have found theropod fossils that have their front limbs spread over nests.

2. Purpose: attraction
Examples: A peacock spreads his iridescent tail to attract a peahen.
Evidence: Scientists have found very small sacs inside theropod feathers, called melanosomes, which give feathers their color and which look the same as those in the feathers of living birds.

3. Purpose: flight
Examples: A bird's feathers are thin and hard on one side, and long and flexible on the other—so they can lift themselves into the air. Modern birds use a moveable bone to pull their wings toward their bodies as they fly upwards.
Evidence: Feathered dinosaurs such as *Anchiornis* had a small, moveable bone that allowed them to fold their arms to their sides. This may eventually have helped them use their feathers to fly.

Exercise D. | Critical Thinking: Evaluating Evidence

- Point out the **CT Focus** box. Encourage students to use these criteria when discussing the questions in exercise **D**.
- Have students answer the questions in pairs before discussing them as a class.

IDEAS FOR...   Checking Comprehension

Ask these questions or write them on the board.

1. What is a theropod and what is known about it? (It is a 125-million-year-old dinosaur that had primitive feathers.)

2. What is *Anchiornis*? (It is a 150-million-year-old bird that had black-and-white arm feathers. Unlike modern bird feathers, the feathers were the same shape on both sides, so *Anchiornis* probably wasn't able to fly.)

3. How do feathers help birds to fly? (A bird's feathers are thin and hard on one side, and long and flexible on the other. To lift themselves into the air, birds turn their wings at an angle. This movement allows air to go above and below the wings. The difference in air pressure allows them to fly.)

4. What do you think is the most interesting aspect of bird feathers? What would you like to investigate if you were researching this topic? (Answers will vary.)

Developing Reading Skills

45 mins

(page 170)

Reading Skill: Identifying Theories

- Go over the information in the box.

- Ask students why it is important to identify signals that indicate that a writer is talking about a theory. (It alerts the reader that the information has not been verified as a fact and is open to question.)

track 2-11

Exercise A. | Analyzing

- Ask students to look at the picture and say what they know about dinosaurs.

- Have students read the information and do the task.

- After checking the answers, you might ask students to read the text again. Lead a brief class discussion: *How would students go about proving or disproving each of these theories? What kind of evidence would they look for?*

Answer Key

Many scientists (think) that <u>a group of dinosaurs closely related to today's birds took the first steps toward flight when their limbs evolved to flap.</u> They (theorize) that <u>this arm flapping possibly led to flying as a result of running or jumping.</u> But recently discovered fossils in China are showing a different picture.

Paleontologists discovered the fossils of a small, feathered dinosaur called *Microraptor gui* that lived between 120 and 110 million years ago. The Chinese team that studied the fossils doesn't think this animal ran or flapped well enough to take off from the ground. Instead, they (think) that <u>this animal possibly flew by gliding from tree to tree.</u> They further (speculate) that <u>the feathers formed a sort of parachute that helped the animal stay in the air.</u>

Not everyone agrees with this theory. Some researchers (suggest) that <u>*M. gui's* feathers weren't useful for flight at all.</u> They (think) that <u>the feathers possibly helped the animal to attract a mate, or perhaps to make the tiny dinosaur look bigger.</u>

Exercise B. | Identifying Theories

When students have finished writing, discuss the answers as a class.

Answer Key

Possible answers:

1. Some paleontologists (speculate) that <u>feathers began as a kind of insulation to keep animals or their young warm.</u>

2. They (think) this shows that <u>the dinosaurs were using feathers to keep their young warm.</u>

3. Scientists (speculate) that <u>feathered dinosaurs such as *Anchiornis* evolved flight by moving their feathered arms up and down as they ran, or by jumping from tree to tree.</u>

IDEAS FOR... **Expansion**

Ask students to find out more about dinosaurs for homework. They could research different theories about why dinosaurs became extinct, for example. Ask them to present their information in the next lesson or to write about it in their journal.

Viewing: Flying Reptiles
(page 171)

Overview of the Video

The video gives information about the paradise tree snake and the Draco lizard. They live in the forests of Indonesia, and both reptiles have developed a way to fly or glide from tree to tree.

Vocabulary Notes

scales = layers of hard skin covering the body of reptiles
dense = thick
flatten itself = make itself flat
twice its normal width = double its size
prey = animals that are eaten by other animals
predators = animals that eat other animals
puffs itself up = becomes larger by filling itself with air
spreads its wings = stretches out its wings
folds of skin = layers of skin that are close together

Before Viewing

Exercise A. | Meaning from Context

- Ask students to look at the picture and say what they know about lizards and snakes.
- Have students work individually or in pairs to match the words and definitions.
- Check answers as a class.

Answer Key

1. dragon 2. branch 3. launch 4. escape

Exercise B. | Classifying

- Allow time for students to use the information in the pictures and the captions to complete the diagram.
- Draw the diagram on the board and invite students to come up and write their answers.

Answer Key

Draco Lizard: has wings, has a long tail

Middle: can fly from tree to tree, live in the jungle, are reptiles

Tree Snake: is long and thin

While Viewing

Exercises A and B.

- Ask students to read the questions in exercises **A** and **B**.
- Play the video. Ask students to check their answers to the Classifying exercise in Before Viewing and to write short answers to questions 1–3 in exercise **B**.
- Ask students to add any new information they learn about the lizard and snake to their Venn diagram while they watch the video.

Answer Key: Exercise A

Draco Lizard
is prey for the tree snake.

live in Indonesia; glide from tree to tree

Tree Snake
can make turns by curving its body into an "S" shape.

Answer Key: Exercise B

1. The tree snake can travel up to 100 meters. The Draco lizard can travel up to 10 meters.

2. The tree snake uses a "J" shape to launch itself and an "S" shape to make turns.

3. The snake is not frightened.

After Viewing

Exercise A.

- Have students discuss and compare answers.
- Play the video again and check the answers.

Exercise B. | Critical Thinking: Synthesizing

Ask students to work in pairs to compare the animals. Then discuss answers as a class. (Possible answers: The dinosaurs may have been similar to the Draco lizard as they might have been able to glide from tree to tree. They were different because they had feathers.)

Preparing to Read

30 mins *(pages 172–173)*

WARM-UP

The Lesson B target vocabulary is presented in context.
Students are asked to identify the part of speech and give
the meaning of the word based on a sentence using the
word in context.

Exercise A. | Building Vocabulary

- Give students time to write their answers and use
  dictionaries to check them.
- Check the answers by asking students to write them
  on the board.
- Point out the **Word Partners** box. Ask students for
  some example sentences using the word *involved*.

Answer Key

1. verb, adapt, change
2. noun, commercial activity
3. verb, part of, connected with
4. verb, copy, imitate
5. verb, partly cover the same area
6. noun, series of actions
7. verb, resist, push away
8. adjective, without a space inside it
9. noun, the outer layer
10. adjective, the only one of its kind

Exercise B. | Using Vocabulary

- Discuss the first question as a class. Make a list of
  possible answers on the board.
- Allow time for students to discuss and write answers
  to the other questions.

Answer Key

Possible answers:

1. rough: carpet, canvas, brush
   smooth: whiteboard, window, table

2. plastic and rubber objects, umbrellas

3. review my notes, practice test questions, work with
   a study partner, memorize key facts or words

4. the change of seasons, learning a new sport or hobby

5. language, intelligence, complex emotions, the ability
   to empathize, reflect, and learn new skills

Exercise C. | Previewing

- Ask students what they already know about these three
  animals. For example, they may know that toucans live
  in tropical regions of South America and eat fruit.
- Alternatively, you can ask them what they would like
  to know about these animals and write a list of their
  questions on the board. (Unanswered questions can
  be done for homework.)

Answer Key

Toucans, beetles, and sharks

Exercise D. | Applying

- Remind students of ways that the architect Gaudí
  used natural forms in his designs (in Unit 8).
- Allow time for students to write their answers
  individually and then compare them in pairs.
- Note: Students will check their predictions in exercise
  A on page 176.

track **2-12**

Ask students to read the passage. Point out the
vocabulary footnotes on pages 174 and 175.

Overview of the Reading

The reading passage describes three animals—toucans,
beetles, and sharks—that have unique features that could
be adapted for the design of new products.

Vocabulary Notes

bill (paragraph B) = beak
mate (paragraph B) = sexual partner
automotive (paragraph D) = car
aviation (paragraph D) = airplane
motorist (paragraph D) = car driver
shell (paragraph E) = hard covering of an animal or insect
figure out (paragraph E) = solve a problem
tent (paragraph G) = temporary home made from cloth
fabric or plastic sheeting and poles
aerospace (paragraph I) = industry that designs
airplanes and spaceships
coating (paragraph J) = covering

Understanding the Reading
(page 176)

Exercise A. | Understanding the Gist

Check students' predictions in exercise **D** on page 173.

Answer Key

The passage is about how unique features of these animals could be used to design products for humans.

Exercise B. | Identifying Main Ideas

Draw the chart on the board and ask volunteers to write their answers.

Answer Key

Animal part	Purpose	Product or technology
toucan bill	Attract mates, cut open fruit, fight, warn predators	To make cars and planes safer
beetle shell	Collect water from desert air	Tent coverings, roofs that collect water for drinking and farming
shark scales	Protect the shark and help it swim quickly	To design airplanes, ship bottoms, and swimwear so that they reduce drag

Exercise C. | Paraphrasing

Check answers as a class. (Possible answer: a process by which characteristics of animals are used to design new products for humans)

Exercise D. | Critical Thinking: Applying

Ask students to explain why these sentences are or are not examples of biomimetics.

Answer Key

Sentences 2 and 3 are examples of biomimetics because they copy nature to make something new. Sentences 1 and 4 are ways of using animal products, not copying their form or structure.

Exercise E. | Identifying Theories

- Remind students of clue words for identifying theories (see Reading Skill box on page 170).
- Point out the **Strategy** box. Ask volunteers to say why these are theories and not facts (because scientists are not sure which theory is correct).

Answer Key

Possible answers:

1. (paragraph B) Charles Darwin theorized that they attracted mates.
2. Others suggest that the bills are used for cutting open fruit, for fighting, or for warning predators.

Exercise F. | Critical Thinking: Synthesizing

Encourage students to look back at the earlier pages of this unit and discuss the different types of adaptations and how they relate to the environment.

Answer Key

Possible answers:

Birds have developed feathers that are adapted to flight, keep them warm, and have different colors that attract mates.

The Draco lizard has developed a long tail that helps it to glide from tree to tree.

The paradise tree snake has learned to make different shapes with its body to help it to glide from tree to tree.

Toucans have adapted to the jungle by developing brightly colored bills to eat fruit and scare off smaller birds.

Stenocara beetles have adapted to the desert by developing shells that collect water.

Sharks have adapted to their water environment by developing scales that help them swim quickly.

Exploring Written English

45 mins

(pages 177–178)

Exercise A. | Brainstorming

- Explain that a summary is a short version of the main facts and does not usually include your opinion.
- Allow time for students to work individually. If students have trouble, allow them to glance back at the reading briefly. Encourage them not to copy directly from the text.

Exercise B. | Journal Writing

- Explain that this task will help students with their writing task in the next part of the lesson.
- Allow time for students to work individually. Offer help or suggestions as needed.

Exercise C. | Analyzing

- Go over the information in the box.
- You may want to bring in a thesaurus or encourage students to learn how to use an online thesaurus to help them understand how to find synonyms.
- Have students complete the sentences.

Answer Key

1. b 2. a 3. b

IDEAS FOR... **Expansion**

Give students further examples of words in the passage that they can find synonyms for.
For example:
enormous (paragraph B) = huge
certain (paragraph C) = sure
spot (paragraph F) = place
inexpensive (paragraph G) = cheap

Exercise D. | Applying

- Monitor students as they work, and help them with ideas if needed.
- Have students share their sentences with a partner or the class.

Writing Skill: Writing a Summary

Go over the information in the box. Ask students which aspect of writing a summary they think is the most challenging.

Exercise E. | Identifying Key Ideas

- Point to the pictures. Ask if anyone owns something that uses Velcro. How does Velcro work?

- Ask students to read the passage first while covering up the right-hand boxes. Then ask volunteers to suggest some key ideas from the paragraph.
- Allow time for students to do the matching individually and then compare answers in pairs.
- Check answers as a class.

Answer Key

a. biomimetics: studying plants and animals to develop products and technologies for people

b. an example of biomimetics: Velcro

c. George de Mestral observed how well a bur attached to dog's fur.

d. De Mestral mimicked the design of the bur and the fur to create a product.

Exercise F. | Identifying Synonyms

- Allow time for students to work individually and then compare answers in pairs.
- Check answers as a class.

Answer Key

a. plants and animals
b. people
c. observed
d. attached to
e. Velcro

Writing Task: Drafting

(page 179)

Exercise A. | Planning

- Go over the steps in this exercise.
- Point out that the topic sentence should be written after the key ideas have been listed.
- Walk around and monitor students as they work. Provide assistance as needed.

Exercise B. | Draft 1

Monitor students as they work, providing assistance as needed.

Writing Task: Revising
(page 180)

Exercise C. | Analyzing

- Ask students to work in pairs to discuss the questions.
- Ask volunteers to explain the reasons for their choice.

Answer Key

Paragraph b is the first draft, and paragraph a is the revision.

Paragraph a is more clearly organized. It starts with a definition and explains the difference between a mutation and an adaptation. It gives examples of each kind of adaptation. All in all, it is a much better and more complete summary of the passage.

Paragraph b does not have a good topic sentence. It does not give a clear example of physical adaptation. It copies many words from the original text. It introduces an opinion with its use of the word *strange*, which a summary should not do.

Exercise D. | Critical Thinking: Analyzing

- Ask students to work in pairs to discuss their answers.
- Go over the answers together as a class.

Answer Key

	a	b
1.	Y	N
2.	Y	N
3.	Y	N
4.	Y	N
5.	N	Y
6.	N	Y

Exercise E. | Revising

- Remind students that asking the questions in exercise **D** will help them to improve their own writing.
- Monitor students as they work. Provide assistance as needed.

Writing Task: Editing *(page 181)*

Exercise F. | Peer Evaluation

- Go over the four steps in the evaluation process to make sure students understand what they are to do.

Exercise G. | Draft 2

Monitor students as they work, and provide assistance as needed.

Exercise H. | Editing Practice

- Go over the information in the box and then have students complete the five sentences.
- Check answers by asking students to read the correct sentences and explain the errors.

Answer Key

1. elegant (*Well-dressed* refers to people's clothing.)
2. light (*Easy* refers to things that are not difficult.)
3. young (*Young* is a collective noun referring to babies.)
4. spread (*Broadcast* is used for media such as TV and radio.)
5. shell (*Bomb* is a kind of weapon that explodes.)

Writing Task: Editing
(page 182)

Exercise I. | Editing Checklist

- Read the sentences in the editing checklist.
- Allow time for students to read and edit their work.
- As you monitor students' work, you may take notes of common errors for later feedback.

Exercise J. | Final Draft

Have students complete their third draft, and then collect their work.

Unit Quiz

- Students can work in groups to answer the questions.
- Encourage students to refer back of the relevant pages of the unit to find the answers.
- To do the quiz as a competition, you can have students work in teams.

Answer Key

1. behavioral	**5.** mimic / imitate
2. Insulation	**6.** toucan
3. theory	**7.** synonyms, antonyms
4. dinosaurs	**8.** keep

IDEAS FOR... Reviewing Vocabulary

Ask students to work in pairs or groups to choose five new words from this unit and draw pictures that will help them to remember the words. They should label the pictures with sentences using the words. The pictures can be displayed on the wall of the classroom.

IDEAS FOR... Journal Writing

At the end of this unit, ask students to write about: a) their favorite animal and its special characteristics; b) what they feel is important for us to learn from nature; or c) an interesting modern design that is inspired by nature.

IDEAS FOR... Further Research

Ask students to research the newest ideas in biomimetics or to find out more about some of the designs mentioned in this unit. They can present the information as a poster or in a short presentation in the next class.

Mobile Revolution

Academic Track
**Business and
Technology**

Academic Pathways:
Lesson A: Taking notes on an expository text
Lesson B: Reading linked texts in a blog
Lesson C: Using a chart to plan a paragraph
Writing a problem-solution paragraph

Unit Theme

How have cell phones changed our lives? How has communication changed since the invention of cell phones?

Unit 10 explores the topic of communication by cell phone as it relates to:

– a software program called FrontlineSMS   – mobile language learning
– radio collars that track lions in Kenya   – a tool for diagnosing medical conditions

Think and Discuss *(page 183)*

- Ask students to cover the caption and describe the picture. What is he doing? What is unusual or surprising about the picture? Have students uncover the caption and check their guesses. Explain that they will learn about how cell phones track animals in the video.

- Discuss questions 1 and 2 and make a list of uses on the board. (Possible answers: to stay in touch with friends, to take and send pictures, to send text messages, to call a taxi) You might make a separate list for smartphones, which you can use to send emails, find map directions, etc.

Note: The Masai are a group of semi-nomadic people living in Kenya and northern Tanzania. They live by herding cattle, goats, and sheep, moving their herds from place to place in seasonal rotation. Much of their land is used for wildlife reserves and national parks.

Exploring the Theme
(pages 184–185)

- The opening spread features a map of the world showing percentage of cell phone use and a chart comparing use of different types of technology, including cell phones between 2000 and 2007.

- Ask students to look at the map and discuss questions A1 and 2.

- Discuss the pictures and say what the people are probably doing and why they are using cell phones.

- For questions B1 and 2, discuss possible reasons for the differences between the increased growth in the use of each type of technology.

Answer Key

Possible answers:

A1. Areas with the densest use of cell phones are North America, Argentina, Europe, Scandinavia, Russia, Malaysia, the Middle East, and Australia. These areas have subscriptions of more than 100 per 100 people, which means that many people have more than one cell phone. Countries with the fewest cell phones include most of Africa and Indonesia. Countries with moderate use of cell phones include North Africa, China, and Turkey.

A2. Answers will vary.

B1. The number of cell phones more than quadrupled between 2000 and 2007. By comparison, the number of phone lines increased by less than a third, personal computers almost doubled, Internet subscriptions almost quadrupled, (but numbers remain small), and televisions increased by 10 percent. Possible reasons for the rapid growth of cell phone subscriptions could be that cell phones are smaller and cheaper than other technologies and they do not require any special technical knowledge to install or use.

B2. Answers will vary.

Preparing to Read *(page 186)*

30 mins

WARM-UP

The Lesson A target vocabulary is presented through a matching exercise. Students are asked to match the new words with their definitions.

Ask students to think of one way that having a cell phone could help health care workers in Africa and farmers in South America. How would the Internet help them? Which would be more useful and which would be cheaper—a cell phone or the Internet?

Exercise A. | Building Vocabulary

- Ask students to read the list of items on the left and match up the definitions they feel sure about. Then have them find the remaining words in the passage.

- Check the answers by asking volunteers to read out their answers.

- Point out the **Word Partners** box. Ask students about the ideas they associate with the word *challenge*. Is it something good, bad, difficult, or interesting? Ask for some examples of challenges students have faced and overcome. Share some examples of your own.

> **TIP** After checking the answers to exercise A, ask students to close their books. Read a definition from the right-hand column, and ask volunteers to say the target word.

Answer Key

1. i **2.** e **3.** c **4.** a **5.** g **6.** d **7.** b **8.** f **9.** h **10.** j

Exercise B. | Using Vocabulary

Invite volunteers to share their answers with the class.

Answer Key

Possible answers:

1. large classes, little or no opportunity to speak with native speakers

2. postal service, public transportation, tax collection

3. studying at a university, becoming a doctor, having a family

Exercise C. | Brainstorming

- Ask students where these places are and have them point to them on a world map. (If you don't have a world map or globe in your classroom, you can use the map on pages 184–185.)

- Have students work in small groups to discuss the question.

Answer Key

1. Africa, El Salvador, South Africa, Nigeria, Malawi, Indonesia, Cambodia, Niger

2. calling a doctor; getting help if you have an accident or get lost; sending information about problems to authorities in a town or city

Exercise D. | Predicting

- Ask students to use the pictures, title, and subheads to predict what the reading is about. Prompt students by asking them to examine the picture at the bottom of page 187 more closely. What can they see? (It shows a woman using a computer to which a cell phone is connected.) What is she doing?

- Note: Students will check their predictions in exercise **A** on page 189.

track **2-13**

Ask students to read the passage on pages 187–188. Point out that the vocabulary definitions in the footnotes on these pages will help them understand the reading.

Overview of the Reading

The passage is about a computer software program invented by a man named Ken Banks. His innovation enables people to send computer information via cell phone without using the Internet.

Understanding the Reading

(page 189)

Exercise A. | Understanding the Gist

Check students' prediction in exercise **D** on page 186. Did they guess the general idea of the passage?

Answer Key

a man who created a software program that allows users all over the world to send information from computers without using the Internet

Vocabulary Notes

run (paragraph A) = organize; manage; be in charge of
voters (paragraph E) = people who choose a candidate in an election

Exercise B. | Identifying Main Ideas

If students have difficulty, encourage them to look at the subheads.

Answer Key

1. He saw that people had difficulty communicating over long distances because it was too expensive for them to get Internet access.
2. It can work with any laptop and cell phone, even when electricity is not always dependable.
3. Nigeria: Voters reported on their election.
   Malawi: A health care program contacts patients to update medical records.
   El Salvador: Farmers receive the current prices for their crops and can earn more money.
4. First, research your idea thoroughly by going into the community and talking to people. Technology is a tool that can help to make the world a better place.

Exercise C. | Identifying Sequence

- Ask students to identify the sequence first without looking back at the passage. Then they can check their answers in the text.
- Ask students to identify the paragraph with this information (paragraph C).

Answer Key   4, 5, 2, 3, 1

Exercise D. | Critical Thinking: Relating

- Brainstorm ideas with the class and share your own experiences. (Possible answers: inviting people to a party, raising money for a charity, getting people to cooperate on a school or community project)
- Point out the **CT Focus** box. Ask students to identify any topics in this unit and in earlier units that they were asked to share their own experiences.

Exercise E. | Synthesizing

- Have students work in pairs. Encourage them to look back through the previous units and review what they have learned.

Answer Key

Possible answers:

Unit 2, page 25 (windmill), page 29 (solar cooker)

Unit 3, pages 45–46 (influence of social media), page 49 (use of social media in Kenya to help economy)

Unit 6, page 106 (use of technology to analyze and classify toxins)

Unit 8, page 148 (use of computer technology to make 3D models of architectural designs)

Unit 9, pages 174–175 (biomimetics, technology that mimics forms in nature to create new products)

Exercise F. | Personalizing

- Help students to brainstorm different technology that could help their community in areas such as health, education, transportation, housing, and crime prevention.
- You may want to assign one topic to each group and see how many ideas each group can come up with, or set a target number of five (or more) ideas for each group.

Ask these additional questions or write them on the board. (Answers will vary.)

1. What do you find most unusual about Ken Banks' idea?

2. What is most impressive about his software program?

3. How is it different from the way many other new inventions are marketed?

4. Can you suggest any other ways that technology can be used more effectively in developing countries?

Possible answers:

1. This software is unusual because it allows local communities to decide how they want to use it, thus enabling change that is initiated by the users themselves.

2. It is impressive because it is easy to use and takes advantage of the fact that many people have cell phones although they may not have computers or Internet.

3. The software is free, unlike many other software programs, and can be used by anyone.

4. Solar-powered laptops, free Internet access.

Answer Key

C	wrote a computer software program called FrontlineSMS	– software sends information from computers using a cell phone – don't need Internet
D	works anywhere	– works with cheap laptops and old cell phones – doesn't need electricity
E	helps people in many countries	– voters in Nigeria – doctors in Malawi – farmers in Indonesia
F	how to turn an idea into reality	– research thoroughly – talk to people in the community – use social media to contact other people with similar ideas

⏱ Developing Reading Skills
45 mins
(page 190)

Reading Skill: Taking Notes

- Go over the information in the box.

- Review the reasons for taking notes using a graphic organizer. Ask if students can think of any other reasons. (It helps you to analyze the information and identify the key points. It helps when reviewing because you don't have to read the text over again.)

- Go over each type of graphic organizer and have students refer back to the relevant pages.

- Discuss which graphic organizers students use most often and why.

Exercise A. | Taking Notes

- Go over the notes in the first row. Point out that these are phrases, not full sentences, and they do not use the same wording as the original text.

- Point out the **Strategy** box. Remind students of the criteria for a good summary (see page 178).

- Allow time for students to work individually to complete the chart.

- Draw the chart on the board and invite volunteers to come up and write their answers.

- Ask the rest of the class to add information as necessary.

Exercise B. | Applying

- Encourage students to use only their notes to write their summary.

- Have students exchange summaries and evaluate each other's work. Were all the main points included?

Answer Key

Possible answer:

FrontlineSMS is a computer software program created by Ken Banks that enables users to send information to large numbers of people from their computers via cell phone. He developed it in order to help communities in developing countries who need to communicate over long distances but do not have Internet access. It helps people in many countries all around the world. Ken Banks advises people with new ideas to research their ideas thoroughly by talking to people in the community and using social media to contact other people with similar ideas.

Viewing: Cell Phone Trackers
(page 191)

Overview of the Video

The video gives information about a new program in Kenya that uses technology to help protect lions. Lions wear radio collars that tell the local people where they are so that the people can move their cattle away from the lions.

Vocabulary Notes

deadly = dangerous
collectively owned = owned by a group of people
remote = far from other people
tasty = delicious
carcass = body of a dead animal
GPS = Global Positioning System, method of locating something using satellite technology
monitor = control, watch
empowered = given power

Before Viewing

Exercise A. | Meaning from Context

- Ask students to look at the picture and say what they know about African lions.
- Discuss the title "Cell Phone Trackers." What does *track* mean? (to search for an animal following the marks they leave behind) What is a tracker? (a person who searches for animals)
- Read the caption aloud and ask students to describe the problem in their own words.
- Allow time for students to work individually and then compare answers in pairs.
- Check answers as a class.

Answer Key

1. nomadic 2. radio collars 3. territory 4. livestock

Exercise B. | Brainstorming

- Allow time for students to discuss in pairs. Then gather their ideas on the board.

Answer Key

The collars send a signal when the lions approach so that farmers can move their livestock out of harm's way.

While Viewing

Exercises A and B.

- Ask students to read the questions in exercises **A** and **B.**
- Play the video. Ask students to check their answers to the Brainstorming exercise in Before Viewing and to write short answers to questions 1–4 in exercise **B.**

Answer Key: Exercise B

1. To keep predators away from the Masai cattle.
2. Money is given to people whose livestock have been killed or injured by lions. In order to receive the money, the Masai have to watch their livestock during the day and keep them behind special fences at night.
3. There are now fewer lion killings on the Mbirikani Ranch than in other areas.
4. In addition to using radio collars and cell phones, Antony is using social media to help to raise money for the project through online donations.

After Viewing

Exercise A.

- Have students discuss and compare answers.
- Play the video again and check the answers.

Exercise B. | Critical Thinking: Synthesizing

Ask students to work in pairs, referring back to the previous reading as necessary, and then discuss the answers as a class. (Possible answer: The lion guardians could send messages to all the herdsmen about the location of lions.)

IDEAS FOR... Checking Comprehension

Ask these additional questions or write them on the board. Play the video again if necessary.
1. Who owns the grassland of Mbirikani Ranch? (It is collectively owned by about 10,000 Masai.)
2. Why do you think the Masai are nomadic? (They follow their cattle as they look for new places to feed.)
3. Why did the Masai kill lions? (To protect their cattle.)
4. How do the lions benefit from the program? (Fewer lions are killed.)

Preparing to Read

30 mins *(pages 192–193)*

WARM-UP

The Lesson B target vocabulary is presented in context. Students are asked to choose the correct meaning and to identify the word's part of speech.

Ask students if they use their cell phones to learn English. What kinds of programs or apps do they have for learning English?

Exercise A. | Building Vocabulary

- Allow time for students to write their answers individually and then compare answers in pairs.

- Check answers as a class.

- Ask students for other word forms of these words. (Possible answers: *(n.)* analysis, *(v.)* apply, *(n.)* empowerment, *(n.)* enrichment, *(n.)* imagination, *(adj.)* imaginary, *(n.)* isolation, *(n.)* practicality, *(adj.)* prosperous, *(adv.)* remotely, *(n.)* transformation)

Answer Key

1. a, verb	**6.** a, adjective
2. a, noun	**7.** b, adjective
3. b, verb	**8.** a, noun
4. a, verb	**9.** b, adjective
5. a, verb	**10.** a, verb

Exercise B. | Using Vocabulary

- Give an example of your own for the first item if necessary.

- Have students write the answers individually and then discuss their answers in pairs.

- Students who finish early can make additional questions using the other words from exercise **A**. For example, *What is an example of something that has transformed your life? What kinds of things do you analyze in your job or future job?*

- Point out the **Word Partners** box. Ask students for some example sentences using these phrases.

Answer Key

Possible answers:

1. more skyscrapers, more roads, more crowded

2. by living in a country where it is spoken

3. by learning a new sport or hobby, by helping other people

4. join a club, meet people online

5. lonely, spacious, quiet, peaceful

Exercise C. | Predicting

- Have students read the first paragraph and the subheads. Ask them to choose the phrase that tells the general idea of the passage.

- Note: Students will check their predictions later, in exercise **A** on page 196.

track **2-14**

Ask students to read the passage. Point out the vocabulary footnotes on pages 194 and 195.

Overview of the Reading

The reading passage describes three innovative ways to use cell phones:

1. to learn English
2. to analyze blood samples
3. to check gold prices

Vocabulary Notes

innovative (paragraph A) = creative
game show (paragraph B) = TV show that is a competition
UCLA (paragraph D) = University of California, Los Angeles
microscope (paragraph E) = scientific instrument that makes small things appear larger so they can be studied
technician (paragraph E) = expert user of a technical tool or device
valuable (paragraph G) = precious, expensive
keep track of (paragraph H) = follow or monitor

Understanding the Reading
(page 196)

Exercise A. | Understanding the Gist

Check students' predictions in exercise **C** on page 193.

Answer Key

The answer is item c. Items a and b are not correct because the passage does not mention cell phone companies, nor does it describe different types of cell phones.

> **TIP** An alternative way of doing the reading is to divide the class into three groups and give each group one of the reading passages. Then team up one student from each group to form groups of three to exchange and compare their information.

Exercise B. | Critical Thinking: Analyzing

- Draw the chart on the board and invite volunteers to come and write their answers.

Answer Key

Problems	Solutions
1. Students do not have time or money to attend English lessons.	learning English by cell phone
2. People live far away from hospitals and doctors.	using a cell phone as a microscope to diagnose medical problems
3. Miners weren't able to sell their gold easily.	using their cell phones to contact buyers and find out gold prices

Exercise C. | Taking Notes

Point out that the chart can help students to identify key ideas and distinguish them from supporting details.

Answer Key

Situation	Solution	Supporting information
Mobile Microscopes	cell phones take a picture of a blood sample	– picture is sent by Internet to a computer in a hospital – computer analyzes the picture of the blood – fewer mistakes
Mobile Miners	gold miners in Choco use cell phones to find out gold prices and sell their gold	– easy to use for miners in remote areas – does not harm the environment

Exercise D. | Applying

- Remind students of the criteria for a good summary (see page 178).
- Encourage students to write their summary without looking back at the passage.
- Monitor students as they work. Provide assistance as needed.

Exercise E. | Critical Thinking: Synthesizing

- Have students work in groups to discuss the questions.
- Ask volunteers to share their opinions with the class.
- Point out the **CT Focus** box. Ask students which of these technologies would be most useful to them.

IDEAS FOR... **Checking Comprehension**

Ask these questions or write them on the board.

1. How are cell phone English lessons different from classes? (You can study alone, whenever you have time.)

2. How does the mobile microscope save time and money? (Patients do not have to travel to a hospital.)

3. Why is it difficult for Chaco miners to sell their gold? (They live in dense jungles with poor infrastructure.)

Exploring Written English

45 mins *(page 197)*

Exercise A. | Brainstorming

- Have students work in pairs to brainstorm a list of problems and solutions using technology.
- Refer students to the problem-solution chart that they completed in exercise **B** on page 196 as an example.

> **TIP** To help students come up with a topic, brainstorm some general topic areas, such as health, education, transportation, crime, farming, fishing. You can assign one topic to each group and ask them to narrow down some specific problems within their topic. Students might prefer to choose a problem specific to their chosen career field.

Exercise B. | Journal Writing

- Remind students that this task will help with their writing in the next part of the lesson.
- Allow time for students to work individually. Offer help as needed.

Exercise C. | Analyzing

- Go over the information in the box. Remind students that modals help to convey how likely or probable we think an action or event is.
- Have students complete the sentences.
- Check answers as a class.

Answer Key

1. could save	3. can help
2. might make	4. will help

IDEAS FOR... **Presenting Grammar**

To help students understand how to use modals to show future possibility, ask them to draw a chart and write 10 things about the future according to how sure they are.

Certain	Less certain	Least certain

Then have students work in pairs and take turns telling each other about the future, using the appropriate modals.

Example: Next year, I will go to college. I may learn to drive. I could go to the U.S. I might get a job.

Exercise D. | Applying

- Monitor students as they work, helping them with ideas as needed.
- Have students share their sentences with a partner or the class.

Writing Skill: Writing a Problem-Solution Paragraph

- Go over the information in the box.
- Ask students to restate the example sentences, using the different model structures provided—for example, *One way to solve the problem of lions in Kenya is to give lions radio collars.*
- Ask students to choose one of the problems and solutions from exercise **B** on page 196 and restate it, using one of the model structures.
- Point out the **Strategy** box and ask students to remember the transition words (e.g., *first, after, next, while, once*), or look back at pages 128 and 136 if necessary.

Exercise E. | Identifying Problems and Solutions

- Ask students to read the paragraph first and then match up the correct labels.
- Ask students to identify the transition words.
- Have students compare answers in pairs before checking answers as a class.

Answer Key

(from left to right)
d, b, e, f, a, g, c

Exercise F. | Critical Thinking: Analyzing

Refer students back to the Writing Skill box. Do students agree that there is about the same amount of discussion for the problem and the solution?

Writing Task: Drafting

(page 199)

Exercise A. | Planning

- Go over the steps in this exercise.
- Help students to choose a problem they would like to write about.
- Review the Writing Skill information on page 198 if necessary.

Exercise B. | Draft 1

Walk around and monitor students as they work. Provide assistance as needed.

Writing Task: Revising
(page 200)

Exercise C. | Analyzing

- Ask students to work in pairs to discuss the question.
- Ask volunteers to explain the reasons for their choice.
- Point out the **Strategy** box. Remind students of clauses of concession using *although.* Ask students to find an example in paragraph a.

Answer Key

Paragraph b is the first draft, and paragraph a is the revision.

In paragraph a, the topic sentence conveys the problem and the solution. There are many details about the problem and a clear explanation for how the solution could work. There is an equal amount of discussion of both problem and solution. The paragraph includes a discussion of an alternative solution and why it wouldn't work. It uses a modal of possibility (*students could pay a lower fee*). The concluding sentence summarizes the problem and the solution.

In paragraph b, the topic sentence mentions the problem but not the solution. There are many details about the problem and there is a lot of repetition, but it does not give a clear explanation of how the solution would work.

Exercise D. | Critical Thinking: Analyzing

- Ask students to work in pairs to discuss their answers.
- Go over the answers together as a class.

Answer Key

	a	b
1.	Y	Y
2.	Y	N
3.	Y	Y
4.	Y	N
5.	Y	N
6.	Y	N

Exercise E. | Revising

- Remind students that asking the questions in exercise **D** will help them to improve their own writing.
- Walk around and monitor students as they work. Provide assistance as needed.

Writing Task: Editing *(page 201)*

Exercise F. | Peer Evaluation

- Discuss the four steps in the evaluation process to make sure students understand what they are to do.
- Walk around and monitor the pairs as they work. Make suggestions and offer ideas as needed.

Exercise G. | Draft 2

Monitor students as they work, and provide assistance as needed.

Exercise H. | Editing Practice

- The purpose of this exercise is to give students additional practice in using synonyms correctly.
- Go over the information in the box and then have students complete the five sentences.
- Check the answers by asking students to read out the correct sentences and explain the errors.

Answer Key

1. With FrontlineSMS, you can **send** a message to many people at one time.
2. Cell phone technology will **make** it easy for people to talk on the phone wherever they are.
3. Online classes could **save** the school a lot of money.
4. New technology may **improve** the lives of people who live in remote regions.
5. I am certain that cell phone-based learning **will** help students in other developing countries.

Writing Task: Editing *(page 202)*

Exercise I. | Editing Checklist

- Read the sentences in the editing checklist.
- Allow time for students to read and edit their work.
- As you monitor students' work, take notes of common errors for later feedback.

Exercise J. | Final Draft

Have students complete their third draft, and then collect their work.

Unit Quiz

- Students can work in groups to answer the questions.
- Encourage students to refer back to the relevant pages of the unit to find the answers.
- To do the quiz as a competition, you can have students work in teams.

Answer Key

1. personal computers
2. reality
3. current prices
4. monitor
5. understand the information better
6. enrich
7. microscope
8. modals, future possibility

IDEAS FOR... Reviewing Writing Skills

Ask students to work in pairs or groups. Ask them to look back through their writing assignments from this book and choose the one they feel is the best. Then they can explain to the group why they thought it was their best work and what they learned from writing it.

IDEAS FOR... Journal Writing

At the end of this unit, ask students to write about: a) why they like or dislike using a cell phone; b) their opinions about using cell phones to learn English; or c) how they think cell phones or other communication technology will develop in the future.

IDEAS FOR... Further Research

Ask students to research recent developments in cell phone technology—for example, in the fields of health or education. Or ask them to research the invention and development of the cell phone. They can present their reports in the next class.

Happiness

Complete the T-chart as you read *Is There a Recipe for Happiness?*

Singapore	Mexico
The government provides _____ _____ and _____ .	People _____ a lot with _____ and _____ .
It has a very low level of _____ , and there is almost no _____ .	Most people live near people in a similar _____ .
Everyone can have a _____ standard of _____ .	_____ , by itself, may not be so _____ for _____ .
Streets are _____ and _____ .	What matters more is how much _____ you have compared to _____ _____ .

Big Ideas

Complete the chart as you read *Big Ideas: Little Packages.*

Problems   **Solutions**

Low-birthweight babies often can't keep

_____

_____.   ➔   The Embrace Infant Warmer _____

_____ .

People have to walk _____

_____ and carry   ➔   The Q Drum _____

_____ .   _____ .

   People can _____ .

   With the pot-in-pot system, the user _____

It is difficult to keep food _____   _____ .

without using _____ .   ➔   The water _____ and

   _____ .

   The health detector device contains

   _____ that are filled

Doctors and nurses have to send _____   _____ . When a person

_____ to _____ and wait   ➔   puts a drop of _____ on the

for weeks _____ .   paper, the chemicals indicate whether the

   person has _____ .

   The StarSight system absorbs _____

   _____ during the day to

In some places it is difficult to get   ➔   _____ at night. The

_____ .   _____ also power

   _____ .

Connected Lives

Complete the diagram as you read *Internet Island*.

❶ The Idea

James's new idea was to create an

_____ and call it a

_____ .

James and Keene wanted their

virtual _____ to become a

_____ .

James's idea came from _____

_____ websites.

❸ The Agreement

Keene and James agreed to pay _____

for a _____ of the island and

$26,500 in _____ to the community.

They also promised _____ for the

_____ .

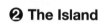

❷ The Island

Keene and James looked for an

_____ for their _____ .

Tui Mali _____ a small island

called _____ in _____ .

He wanted someone to _____

his _____ , so he decided to

_____ on the _____ .

Keene and James _____ him.

❹ The Tribe

In September of 2006, Keene and 13 of his

_____ members _____

to _____ . They worked with

the _____ tribe members and

built _____ , planted _____ , and

set up non-polluting sources of _____

such as _____ . They

became _____ and one _____ .

Deep Trouble

Complete the reporter's notes as you read *An Interview with Barton Seaver*.

Barton Seaver: a _____ and _____

who wants to save _____ .

He believes people's choices for _____ have a direct

_____ on the _____ health.

He doesn't believe we should stop _____ altogether—but,

we should avoid eating species that have been severely _____ .

His advice about what to eat:

- We should eat _____ and _____ that are low on

   _____ and can be harvested with _____ impact on

   the _____ (for example: farmed mussels,

   _____ and oysters, anchovies, _____ , and herring).

- We should not eat _____ fish (like _____ , orange roughy,

   _____ , sturgeon, and _____).

He believes the health of the _____ is directly related to the

health of _____ because the ocean . . .

- provides the _____ we _____

- has a big effect on the _____

- provides a necessary and vital _____ for billions of people.

Memory and Learning

Complete the T-chart as you read *The Art of Memory*.

The Art of Memory: in the past	The Art of Memory: now
About 2,500 years ago: Simonides of Ceos discovered a powerful memory technique called the _____ _____ . According to the method, if you _____ certain things in a familiar _____ , you can keep them in your _____ for a long time. Simonides called this imagined place a _____ . In 15th-century Italy: Peter of Ravenna used this method to _____ books and poems.	In the 20th and 21st centuries: We've gradually replaced our _____ memory with _____ memory. We've invented _____ so we don't have to store _____ in our _____ . For example, we have: _____ to record our experiences; _____ to keep track of our schedules; _____ and the _____ to store our collective _____ .

Dangerous Cures

Use the Venn diagram to compare Leon Fleisher and Karen Wetterhahn as you read *Poison and the Piano Player and A Dangerous Job*. How are they different? What is similar about them?

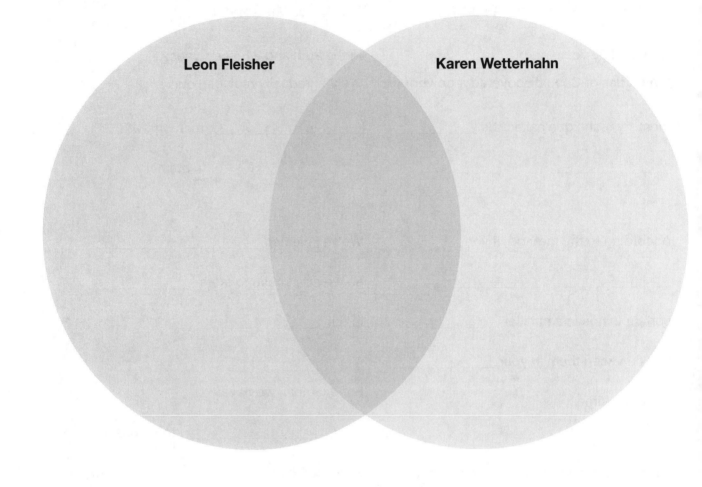

Leon Fleisher

Karen Wetterhahn

Nature's Fury

Complete the notes as you read *What to Do When a Tornado Strikes.*

Before

First, pay attention to _____
during _____ .
In addition, keep your _____
on the _____ . Watch
for _____ , greenish-colored
_____ , and clouds that are
_____ the _____ .
As soon as you know a _____
is about to _____ , find
_____ immediately if you
are _____ . If you are
_____ , go to the lowest
_____ you _____ ,
for example, to a _____ .

During

Once the tornado _____ ,
stay _____ for the _____
_____ . **During a tornado**,
stay _____ from _____ ,
as tornadoes can _____ them
to _____ .

After

When the storm is _____ ,
make sure _____ are
_____ . Check your
_____ and the _____
around it for _____ . **Finally**,
contact _____ relief _____
for _____ with _____
and other _____ such
as _____ and _____ .

Building Wonders

Complete the timeline as you read *Unfinished Masterpiece*.

1852
Antoní Gaudí _____ near Reus, Spain.

Gaudí began _____ his church, _____ .

1893
The _____ stage of church was _____ .

Gaudí stopped _____ on any _____ projects.

1926
Gaudí _____ . He made three-dimensional _____ so that others could _____ his masterpiece.

1935-1939
Many of Gaudí's models were _____ during the _____ , but some _____ .

2020
The church's main _____ will be _____ .

All _____ on La Sagrada Família is _____ to be finished.

Form and Function

Complete the information about the three animals as you read *Design by Nature*.

Toucan ___bills___

Description	Used for	Human applications
- designed to be both strong and _____ - outside made of layers of overlapping _____ - _____ has a foam-like structure - design makes the bill _____ but very _____	- attracting _____ - cutting open _____ - fighting, or for warning _____ to stay _____	- can use design of the toucan bill to make _____ and _____ safer - may protect _____ involved in _____

Stenocara beetle _____

Description	Used for	Human applications
- surface is covered with _____ - top of each bump is _____ and attracts _____ - sides and areas in _____ the bumps _____ water	- collecting _____ the desert _____	- shell is a good _____ for designing inexpensive _____ coverings - might also be a model for _____ that can collect water for _____ and _____

Shark _____

Description	Used for	Human applications
- are made from the same _____ as _____ - are flexible	- protecting the shark - helping it _____ quickly - helping it reduce the water's _____	- can inspire designs for _____ , like _____ , that experience _____ - coating _____ bottoms - designing _____

Mobile Revolution

Complete the chart as you read *Changing the World with a Cell Phone.*

Problems	Solutions
It was difficult for organizations in Africa to _____ over great _____ .	Ken Banks created computer _____ called FrontlineSMS. It allows users to send information from _____ without using the _____ .
Nigerians wanted to monitor their _____ in 2007.	Voters used Frontline SMS to send 10,000 _____ to describe what was happening when they went to _____ .
It is difficult and expensive for a rural _____ care program in Malawi to contact _____ .	Program workers use Frontline SMS to _____ patients, so they don't have to visit patients' _____ to update _____ records. The program saves doctor _____ and _____ costs.
It is difficult for _____ in Indonesia, Cambodia, Niger, and El Salvador to get current _____ for their _____ .	Farmers use Frontline SMS to receive the most _____ prices for their crops by _____ , so they can _____ more money.